History of the Great War.

MILITARY OPERATIONS.

HISTORY OF THE GREAT WAR
BASED ON OFFICIAL DOCUMENTS
BY DIRECTION OF THE HISTORICAL SECTION OF THE
COMMITTEE OF IMPERIAL DEFENCE

MILITARY OPERATIONS EGYPT & PALESTINE

1914–1918

ATLAS

The Naval & Military Press Ltd

Published by

The Naval & Military Press Ltd
Unit 5 Riverside, Brambleside
Bellbrook Industrial Estate
Uckfield, East Sussex
TN22 1QQ England

Tel: +44 (0)1825 749494

www.naval-military-press.com
www.nmarchive.com

In reprinting in facsimile from the original, any imperfections are inevitably reproduced and the quality may fall short of modern type and cartographic standards.

Sketches and Maps
Volume 1

Sketch A	The Western Desert	....	12
,, B	The Eastern Desert	....	14
,, 1.	Attack on Suez Canal, 3rd February 1915..	....	17
,, 2.	Affair of the Wadi Senab, 11th/13th December 1915	....	18
,, 3.	Affair of the Wadi Majid, 25th December 1915	....	19
,, 4.	Affair of Halazin, 23rd January 1916	....	20
,, 5.	Action of Agagiya, 26th February 1916	....	21
,, 6.	Operations at Girba and Siwa, 3rd/4th February 1917	....	22
,, 7.	Operations against the Sultan of Darfur, March–December 1916 ..	....	23
,, 8.	Affair of Qatiya, 23rd April 1916..	....	24
,, 9.	Turkish Railway Communications, August 1916	....	25
,, 10.	Battle of Romani, August 1916 ..	....	26
,, 11.	Arabia and Syria, June 1916 ..	....	27
,, 12.	Affair of Magdhaba, 23rd December 1916	....	28
,, 13.	Action of Rafah, 9th January 1917..	....	29
,, 14.	First Battle of Gaza, 26th March, 1917	....	30
,, 15.	First Battle of Gaza, 27th March 1917	....	31
,, 16.	Second Battle of Gaza, 19th April 1917	....	32
Diagram I.	Water Supply, Eastern Frontier Force, November 1916	....	34
,, II.	The Sinaitic Peninsula (5 Sections)	....	35

Sketches and Maps
Volume 2 Part 1

Sketch A.	The Judæan Fortress	....	36
,,	1. Third Gaza, 6 p.m. 28th October 1917	....	39
,,	2. Third Gaza, 6 p.m. 31st October 1917	....	40
,,	3. Capture of Beersheba, 31st October 1917	....	41
,,	4. Third Gaza, 6 p.m. 1st November 1917	....	42
,,	5. Third Gaza, 6 p.m. 3rd November 1917	....	43
,,	6. Third Gaza, 6 p.m. 6th November 1917	....	44
,,	7. Affair of Huj, 8th November 1917 ..	....	45
,,	8. Wadi el Hesi, 8th November 1917 ..	....	46
,,	9. Third Gaza, 6 p.m. 10th November 1917	....	47
,,	10. Capture of Junction Station, 13th–14th November 1917	....	48
,,	11. Action of El Maghar, 13th November 1917	....	49
,,	12. Jerusalem Operations, 6 p.m. 19th November 1917	....	50
,,	13. Battle of Nabi Samweil, 6 p.m. 21st November 1917	....	51
,,	14. Turkish Counter-offensive, 6 p.m. 28th November 1917	....	52
,,	15. Wilhelma, 27th November 1917 ..	....	53
,,	16. Turkish Attack, 28th November 1917	....	54
,,	17. Attack on Beit 'Ur el Foqa, 29th–30th November 1917	....	55
,,	18. Capture of Jerusalem, 6 p.m. 7th December 1917	....	56
,,	18A. Jerusalem	....	57
,,	19. Capture of Jerusalem, 8th–9th December 1917	....	58
,,	20. Passage of Nahr el 'Auja, 20th–21st December 1917	....	59
,,	21. Defence of Jerusalem, 6 p.m. 30th December 1917	....	60

Sketch 22.	Capture of Jericho, 19th–21st February 1918	.. .. ..	61
,, 23.	Tell 'Asur, 230th Brigade, 8th–10th March 1918 ..	.. .. ..	62
,, 24.	Theatre of Operations in Trans-Jordan		64
,, 25.	'Amman, 30th March 1918 ..	..	65
,, 26.	Turkish Attack on Jordan Bridgeheads, 11th April 1918	.. ..	67
Diagram I.	Palestine : the Lie of the Land	..	68
,, II.	Outline of Ground around the Holy City..	.. ..	69

Volume 2 Part 2

Sketch 27.	Et Tafila, 25th January 1918	..	71
,, 28.	Affair of Abu Tulul, 14th July 1918 ..		72
,, 29.	Abu Tulul, Cavalry Operations, 14th July 1918	.. ..	73
,, 30.	Megiddo, Zero Hour 19th September 1918 ..	.. ..	74
,, 31.	Megiddo, Midnight 19th–20th September 1918	.. ..	75
,, 32.	Megiddo, 9 p.m. 20th September 1918		76
,, 33.	Megiddo, 9 p.m. 21st September 1918 ..	.. ..	77
,, 34.	Capture of Haifa, 23rd September 1918 ..	.. ..	78
,, 35.	Megiddo, 9 p.m. 24th September 1918		79
,, 36.	Action at Makhadet el Mas'udi, 24th September 1918	.. ..	80
,, 37.	Capture of Samakh, 25th September 1918 ..	.. ..	81
,, 38.	Arab Raids and 4th Cav. Division, 16th–17th September 1918	..	82
,, 39.	Advance to Damascus, 29th–30th September 1918	.. .. ..	83
,, 40.	Attack on Irbid, 26th September 1918 ..	.. ..	84
,, 41.	Pursuit from Damascus to Aleppo, 1st–28th October 1918	.. ..	85
,, 42.	Administration of Occupied Territory		86
,, 43.	Affair of Haritan, 26th October, 1918		87

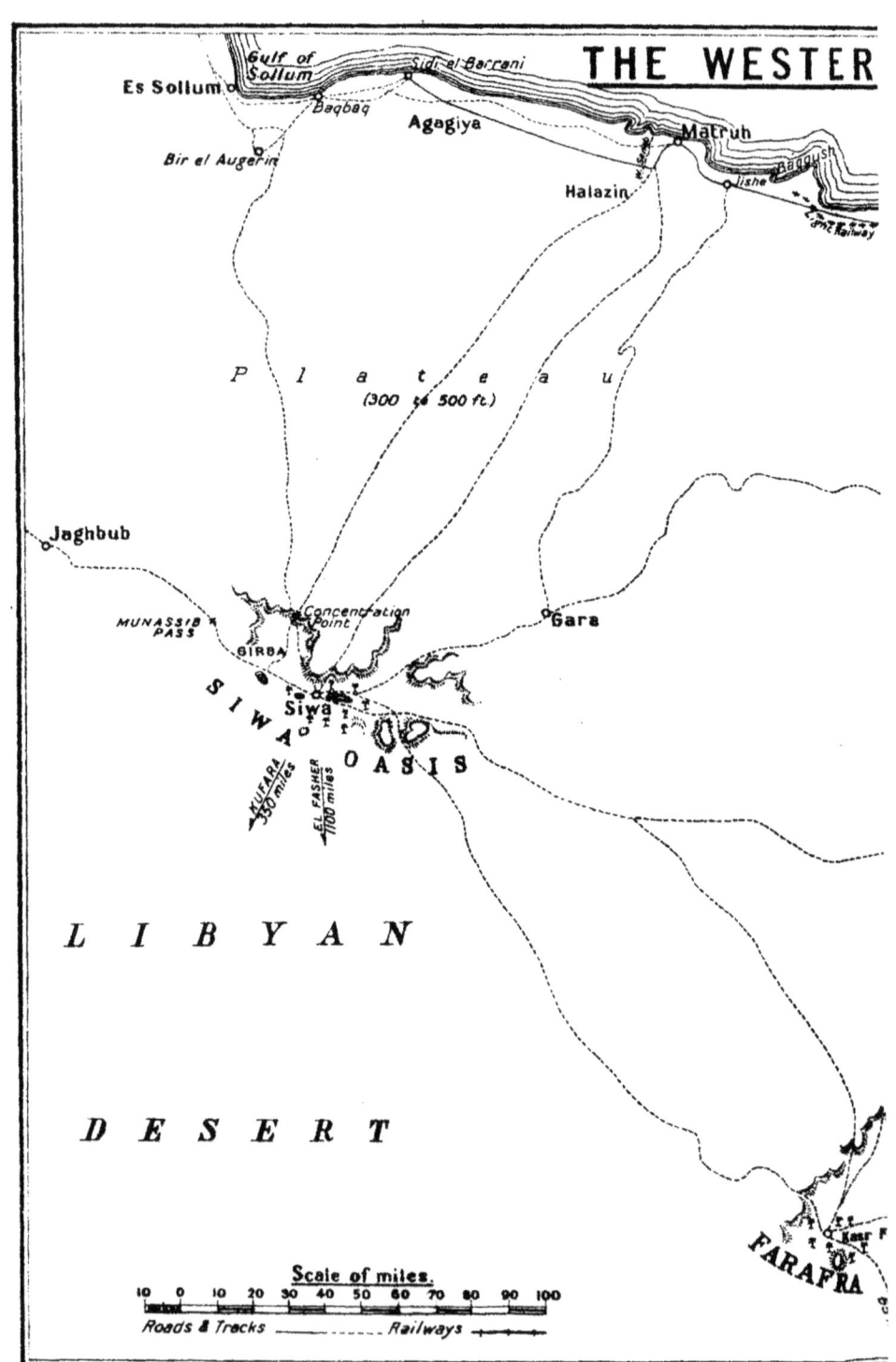

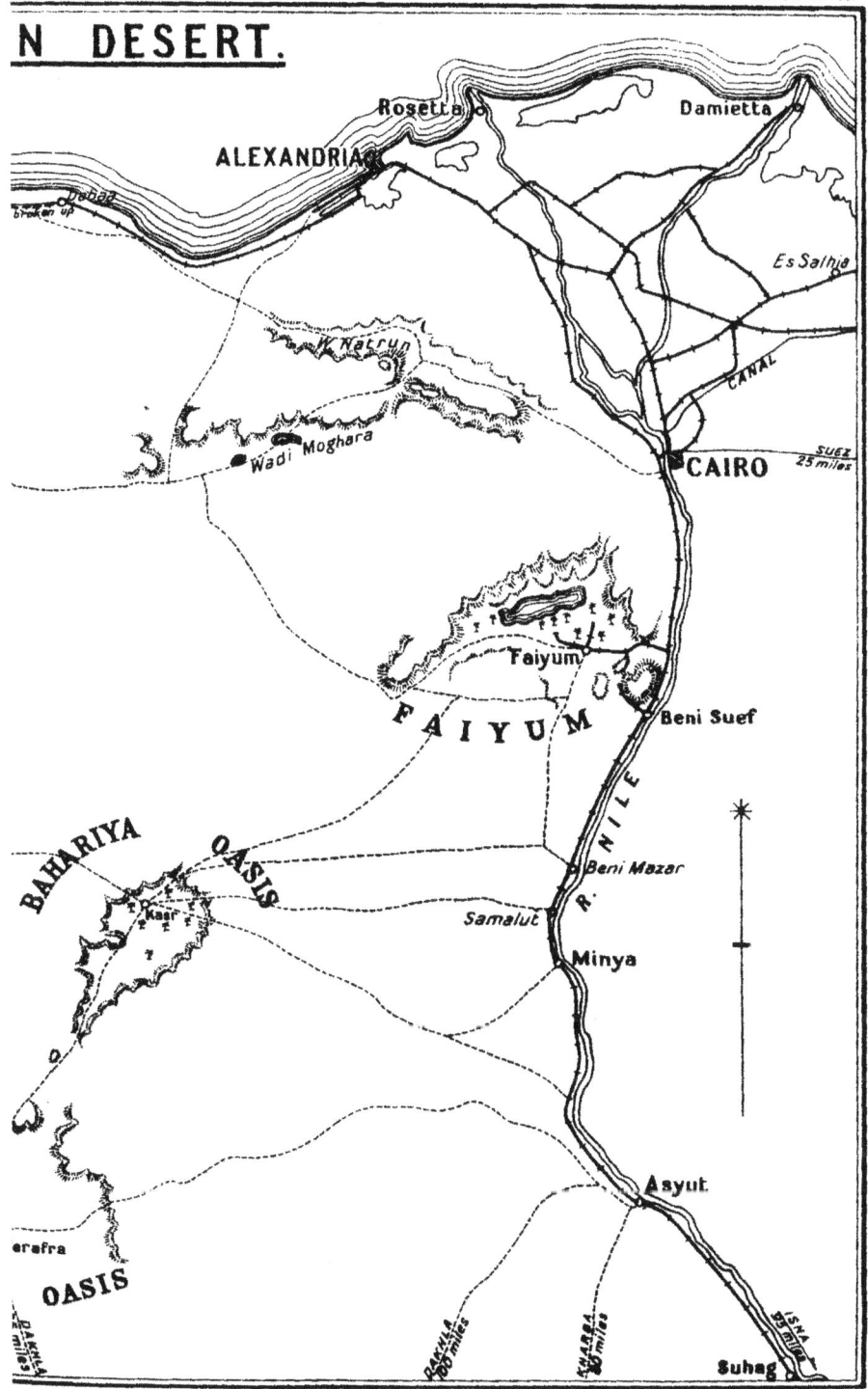

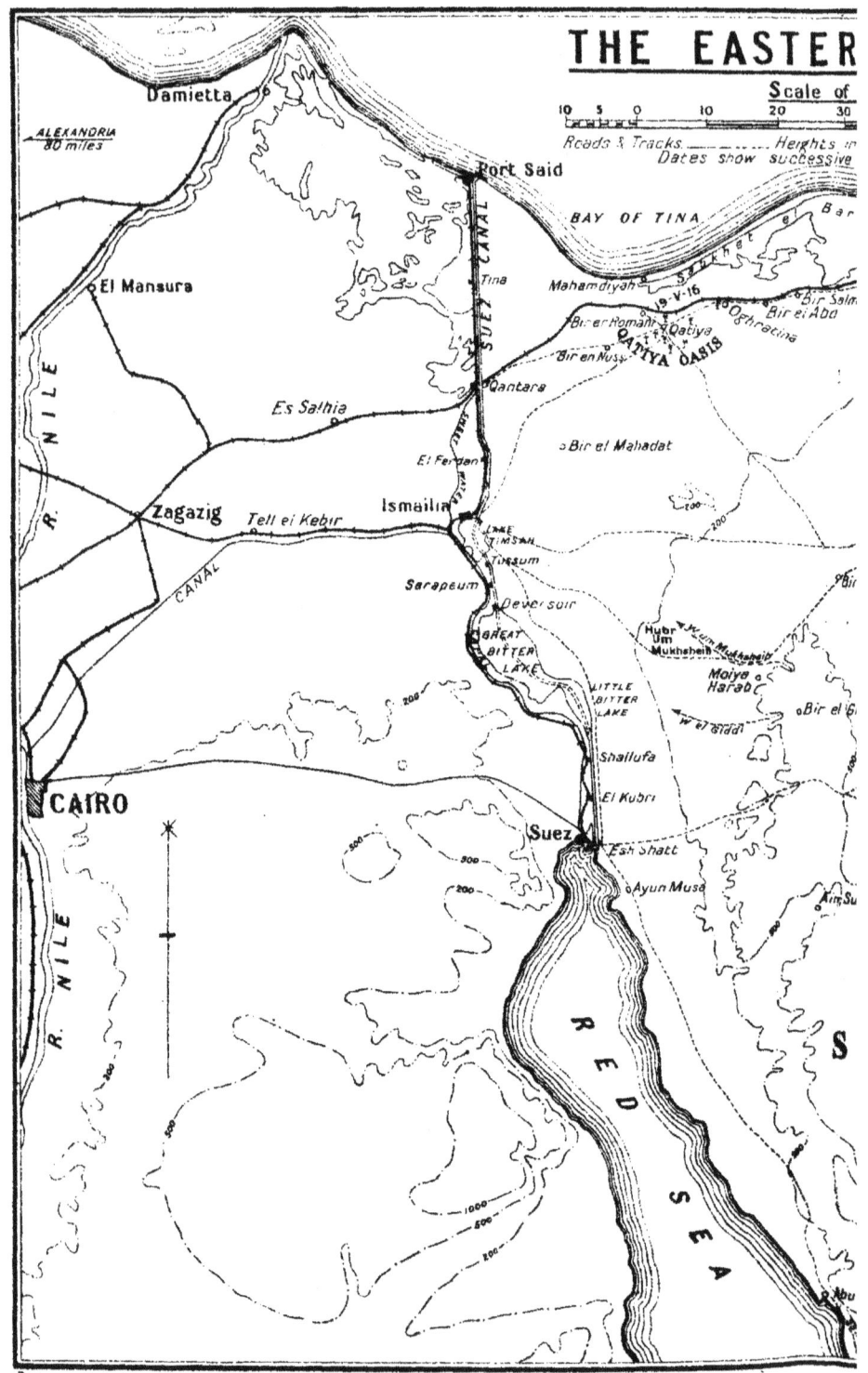

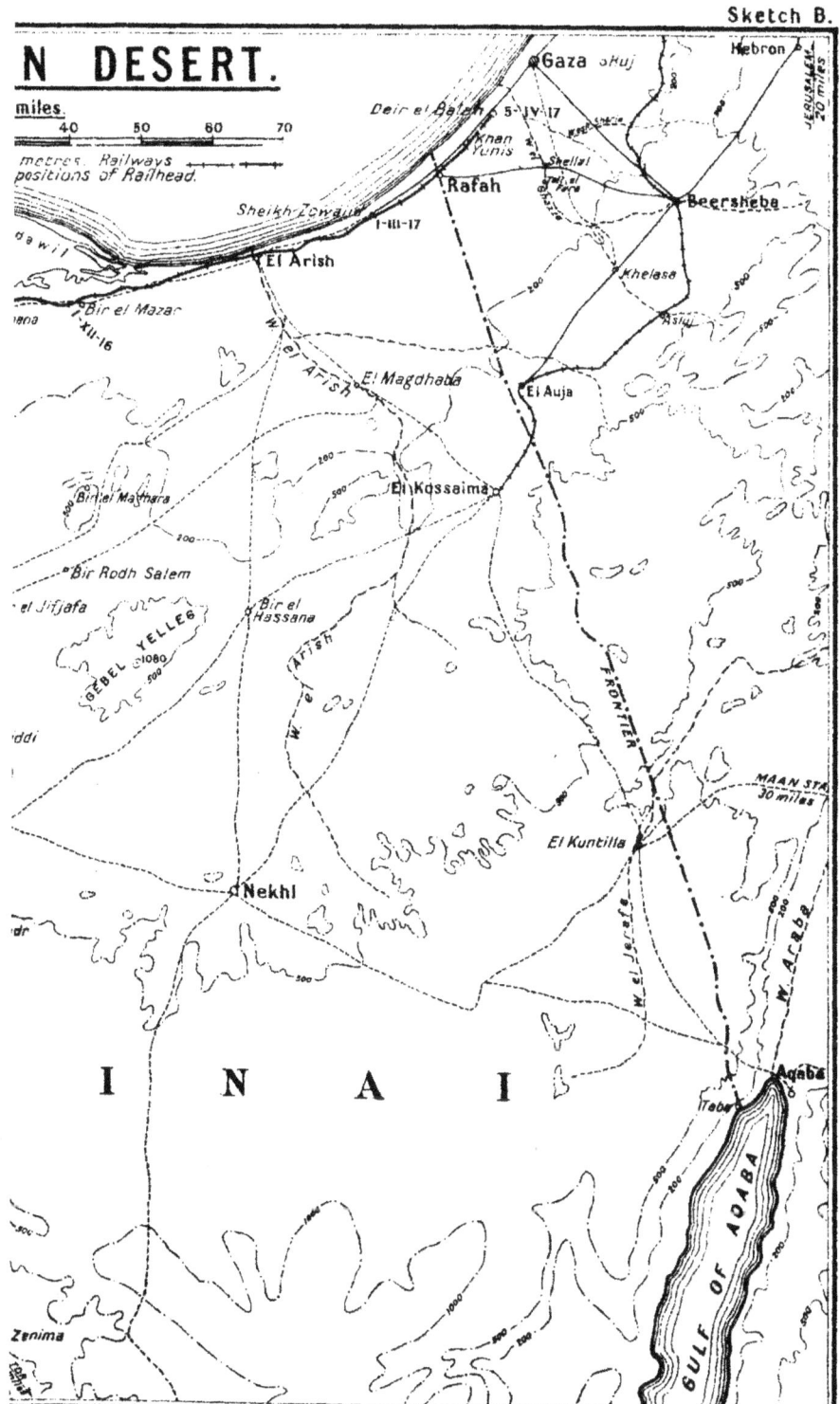

Sketch 1.

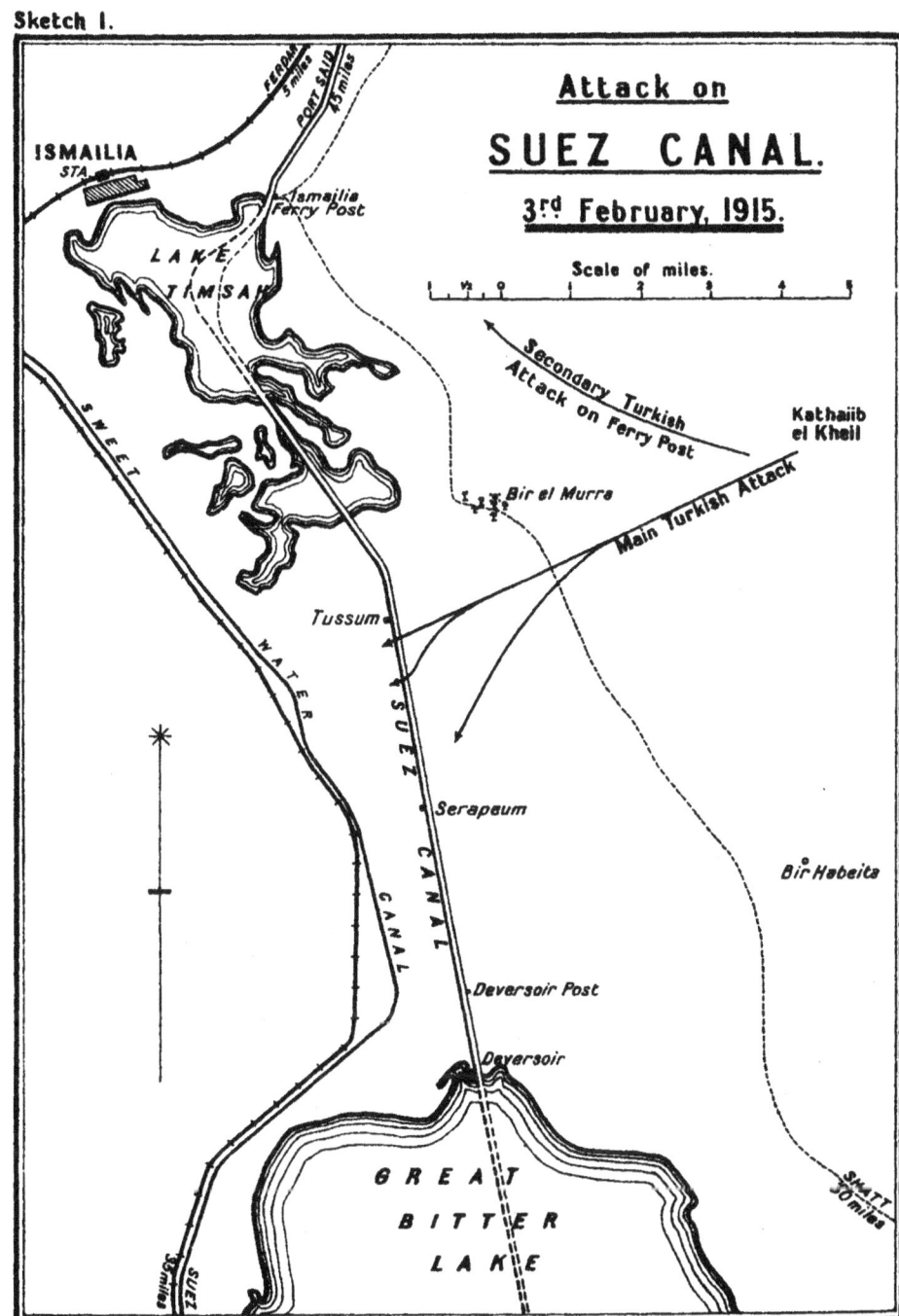

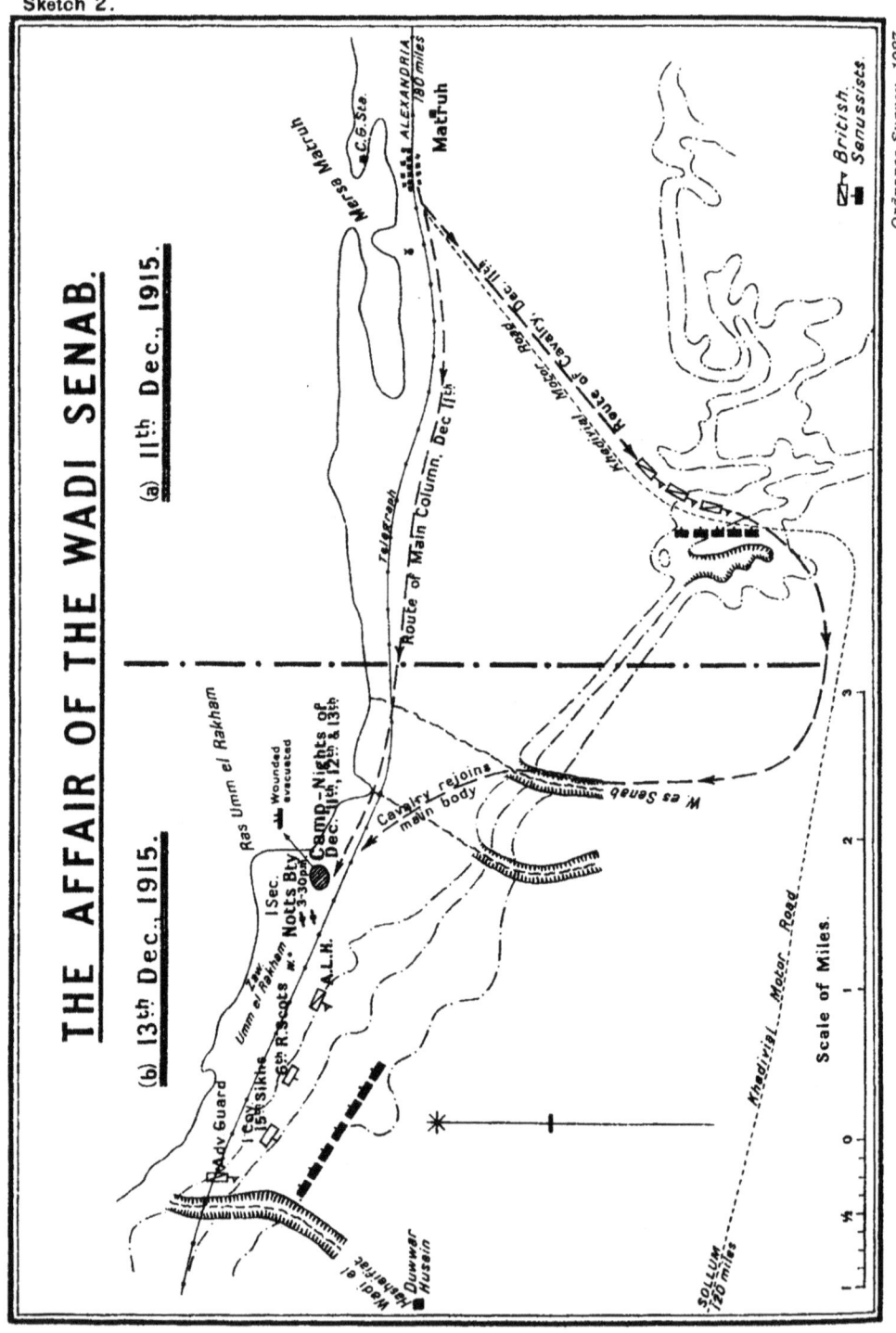

Sketch 3

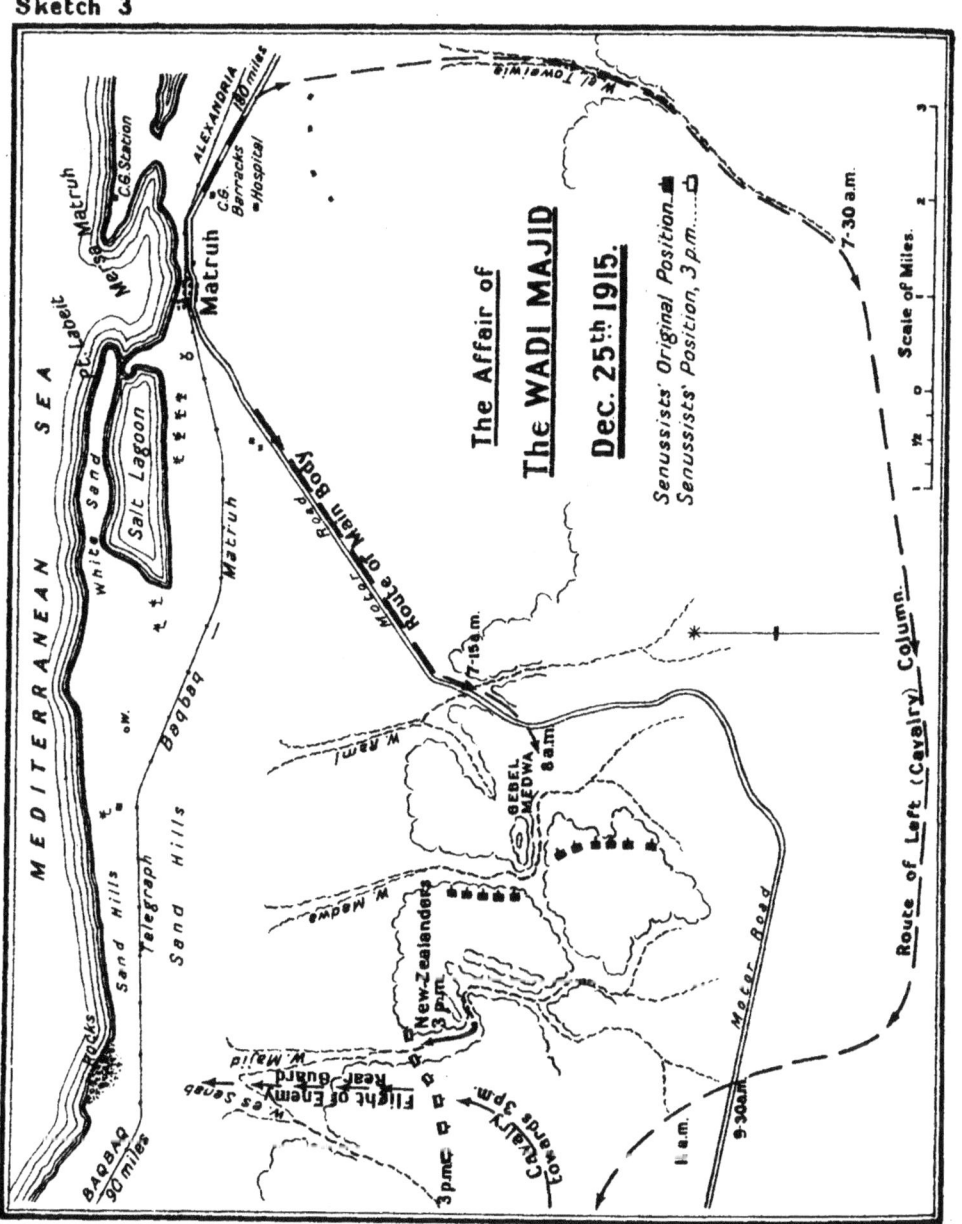

Sketch 4.

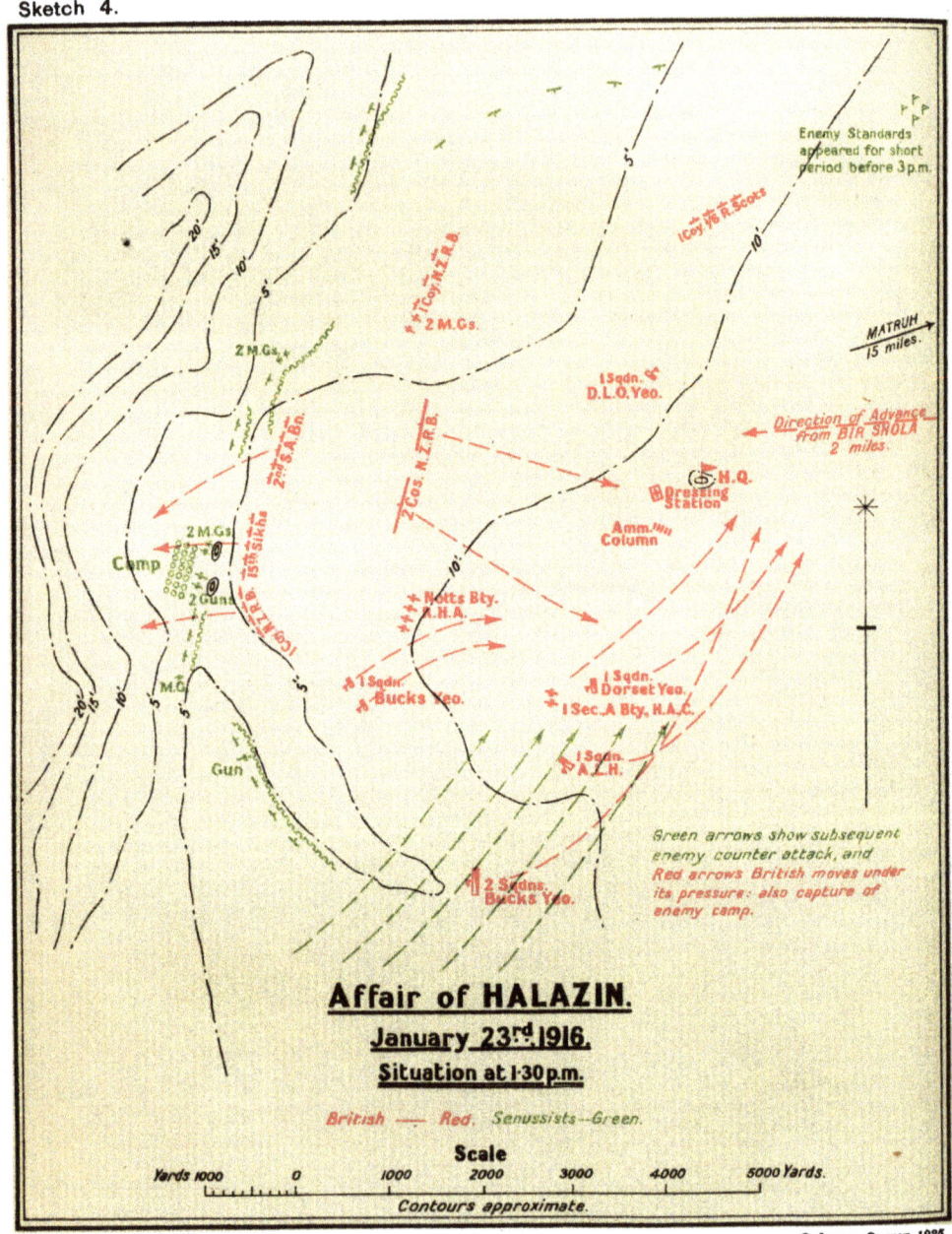

Sketch 5.

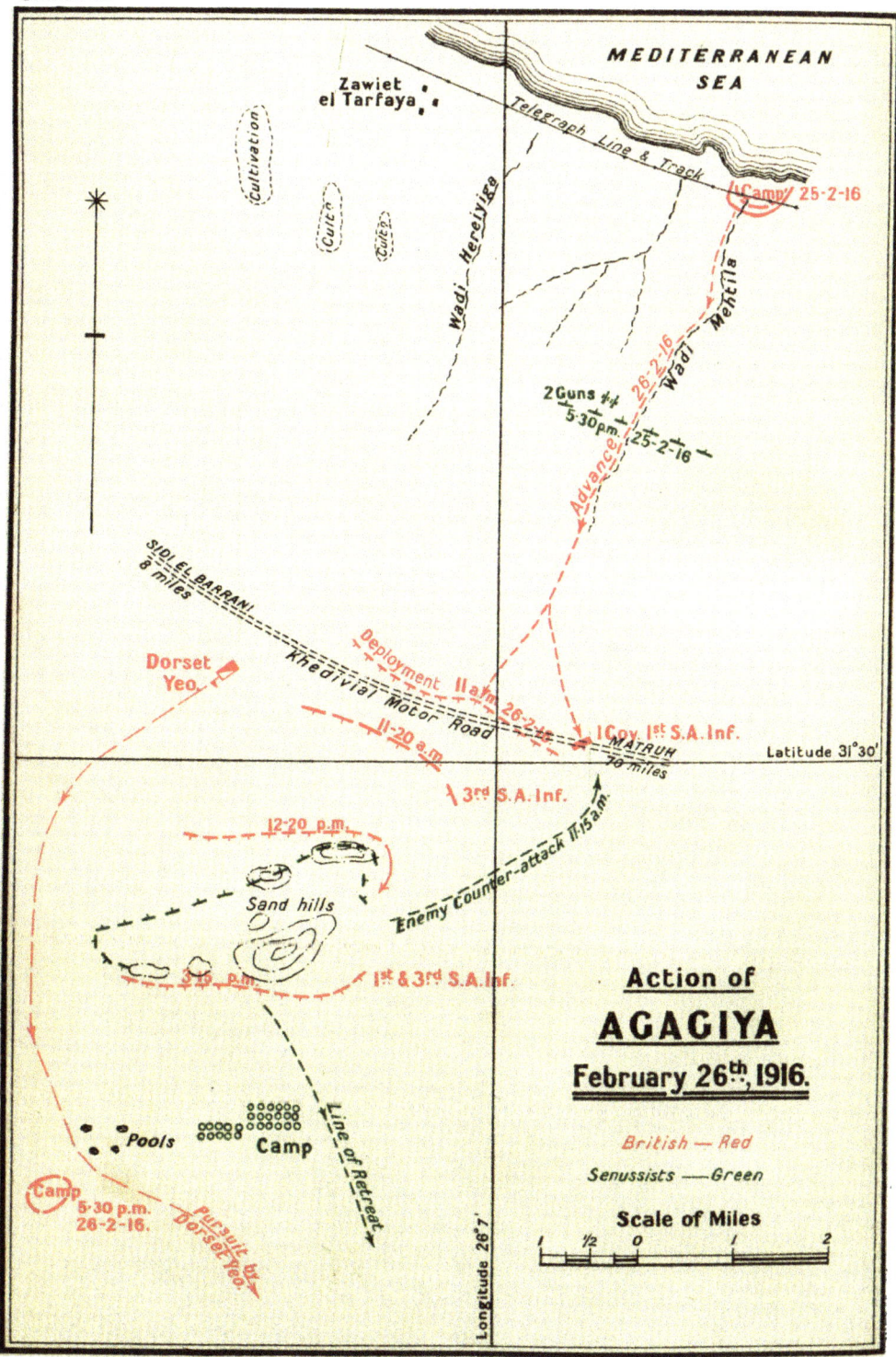

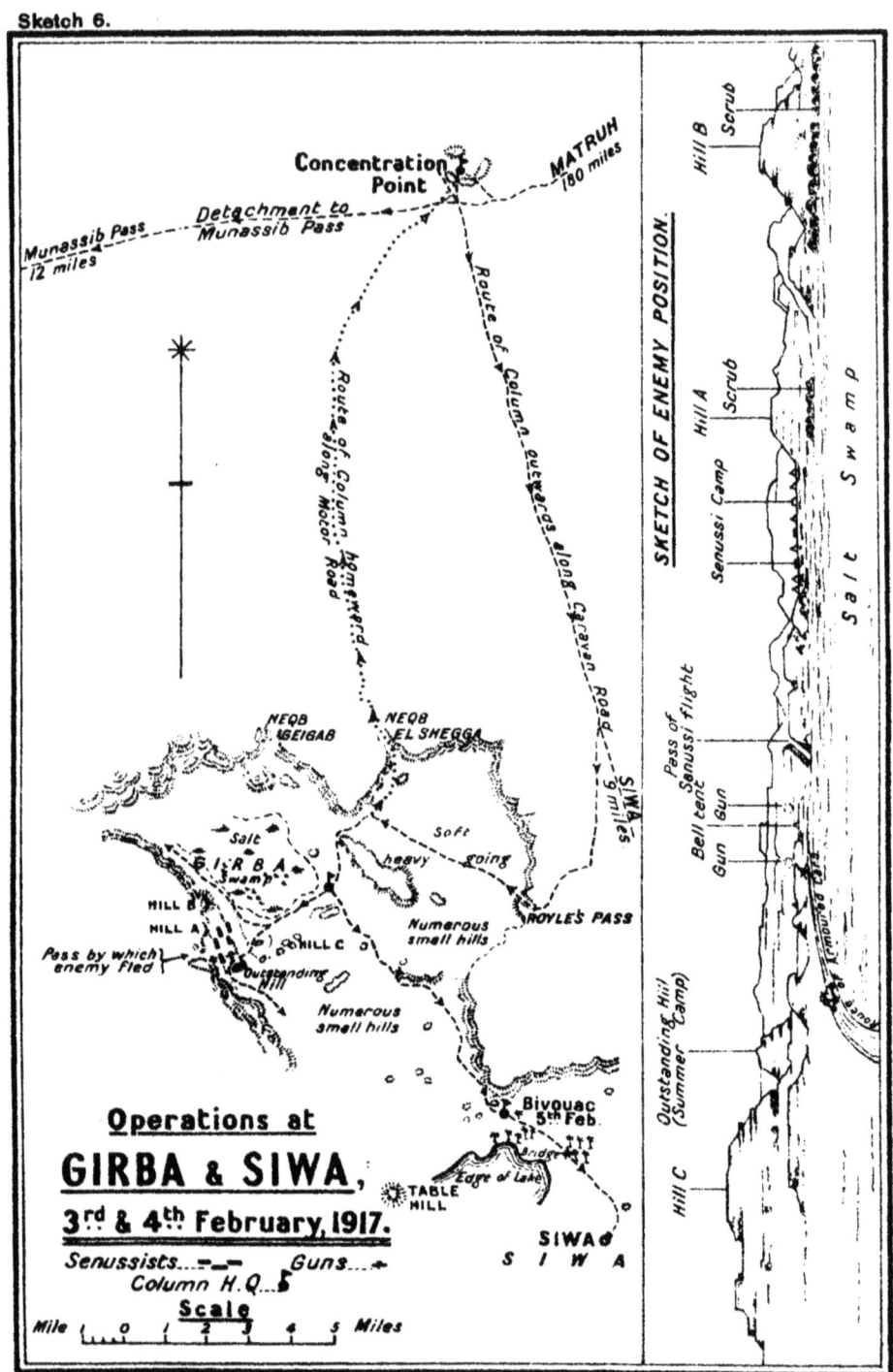

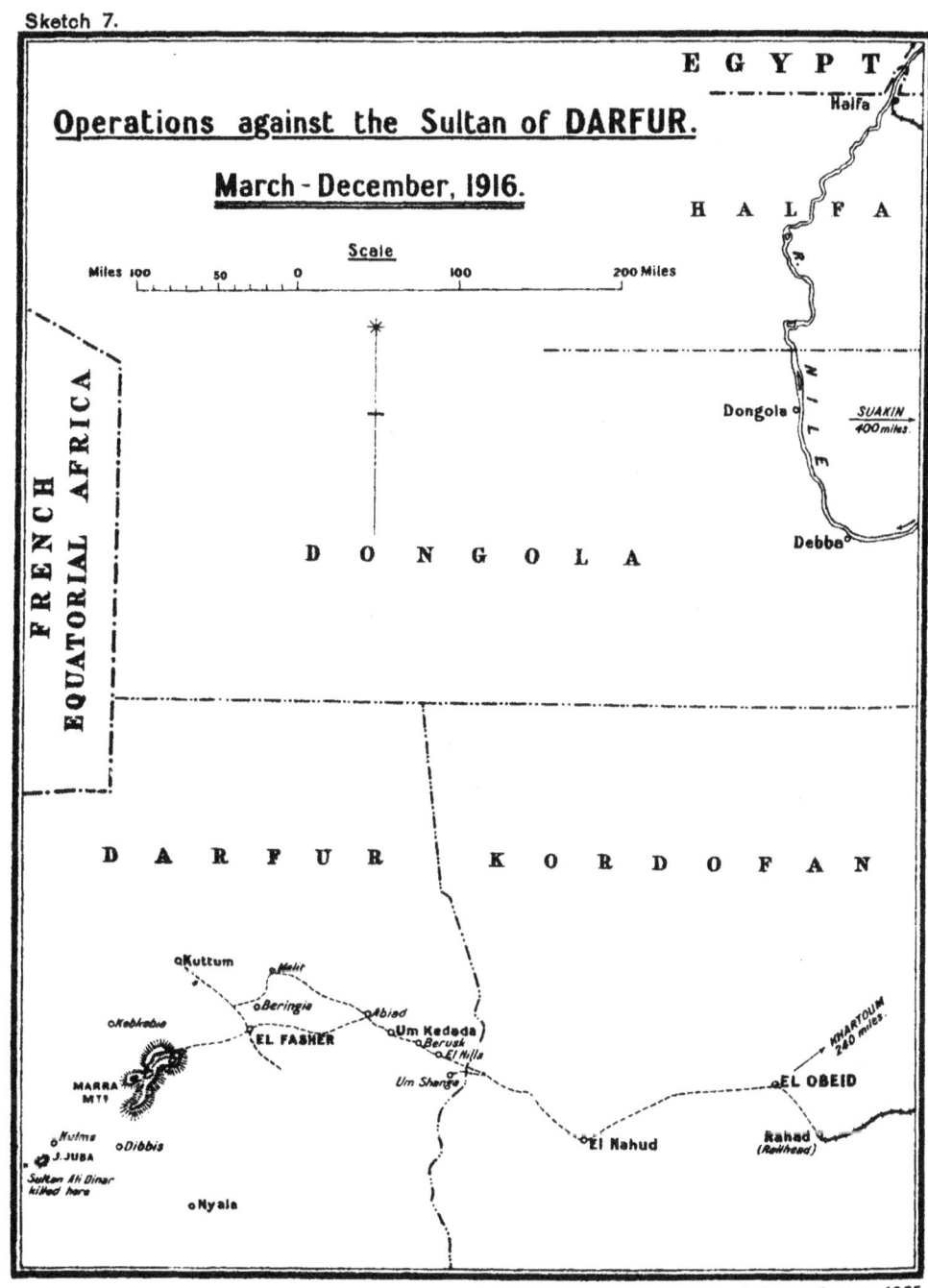

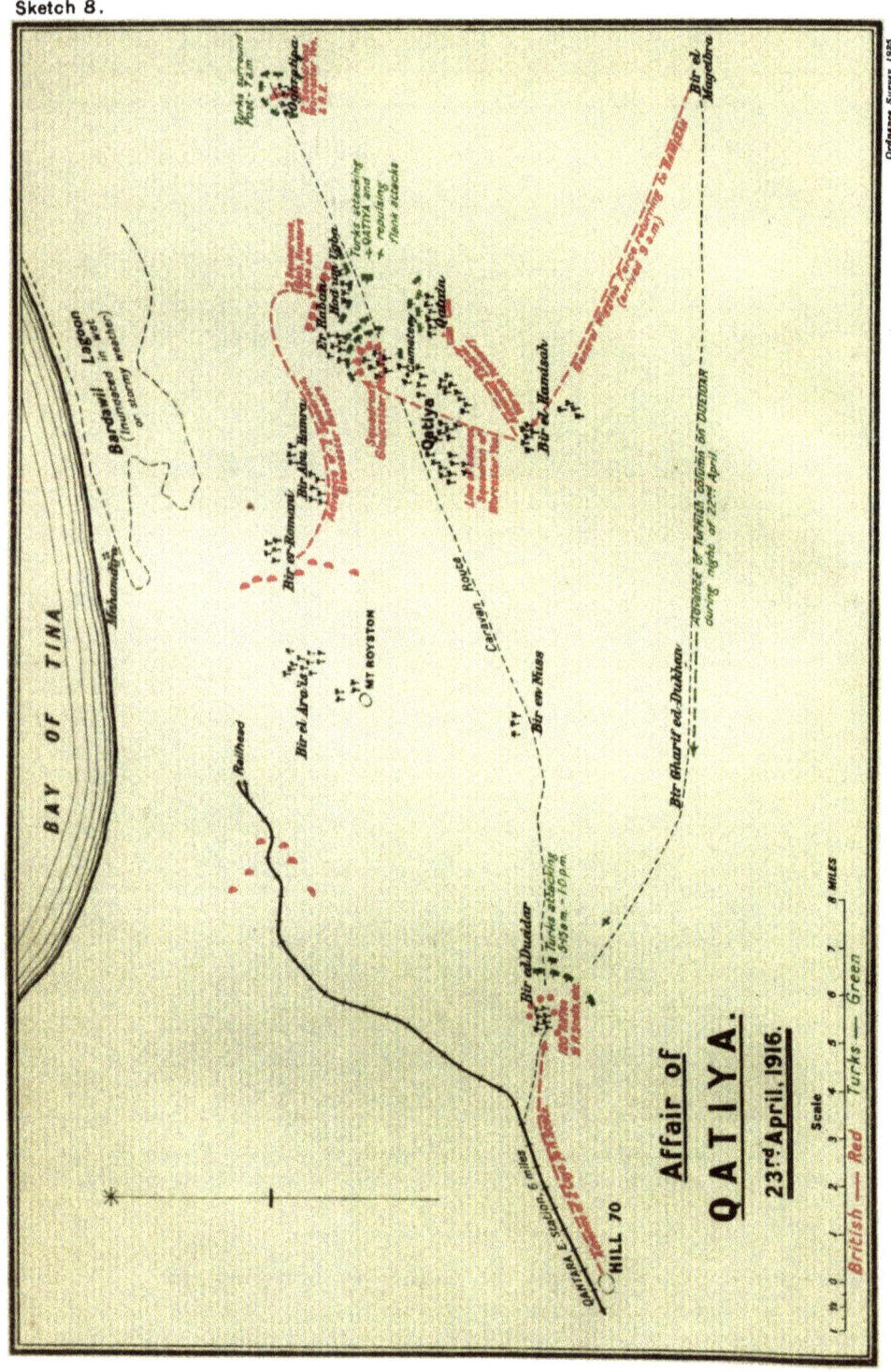

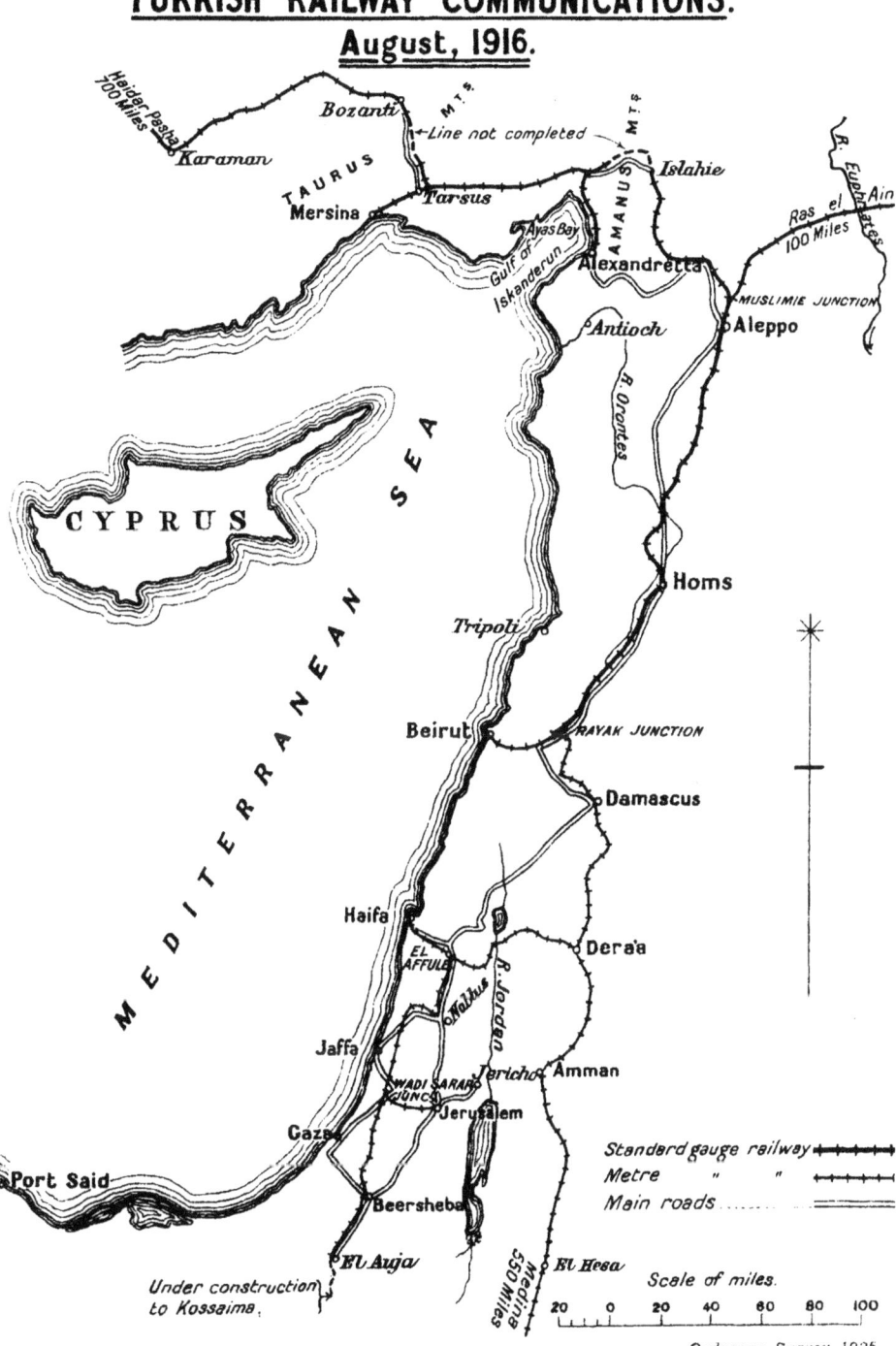

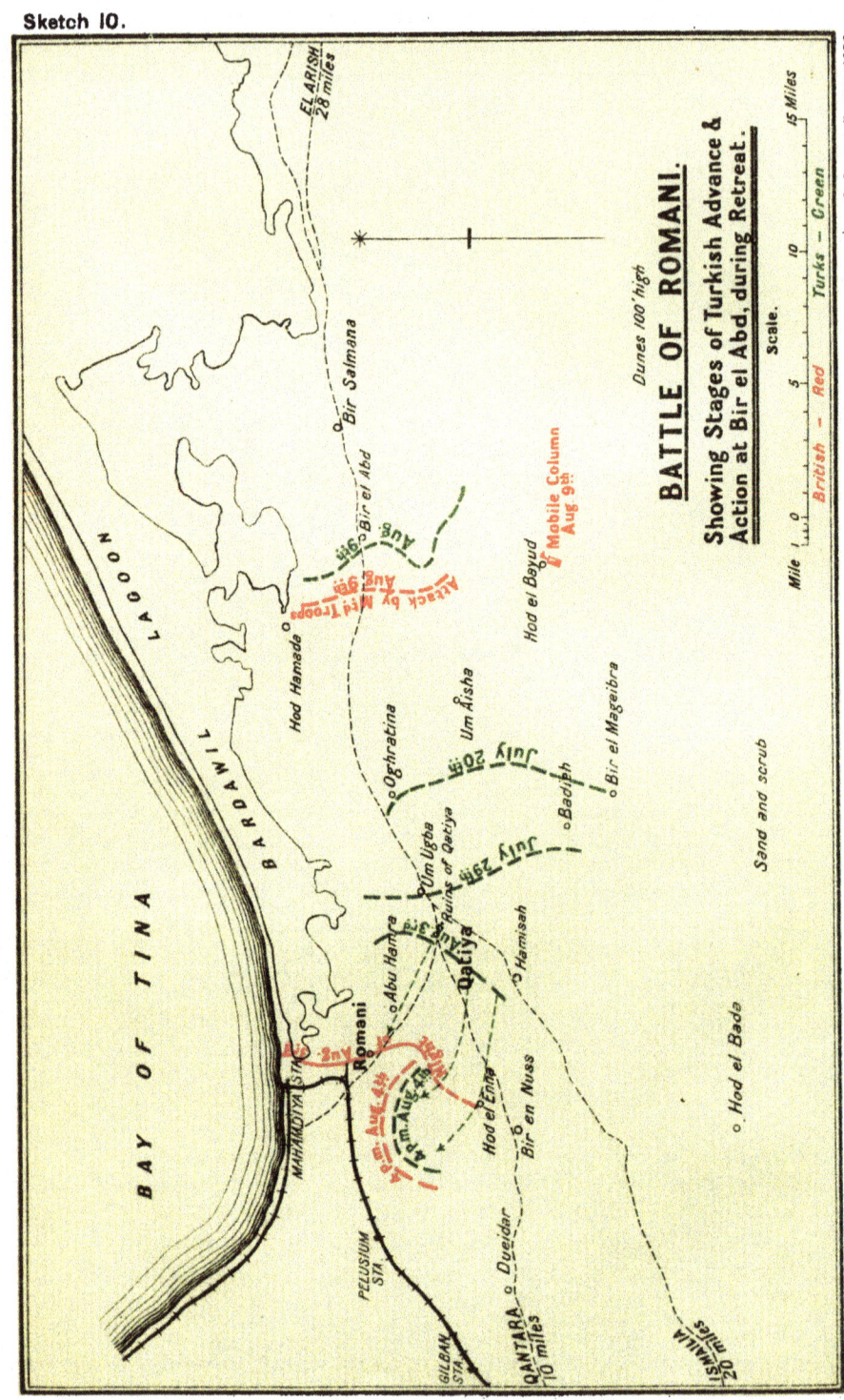

Sketch II.

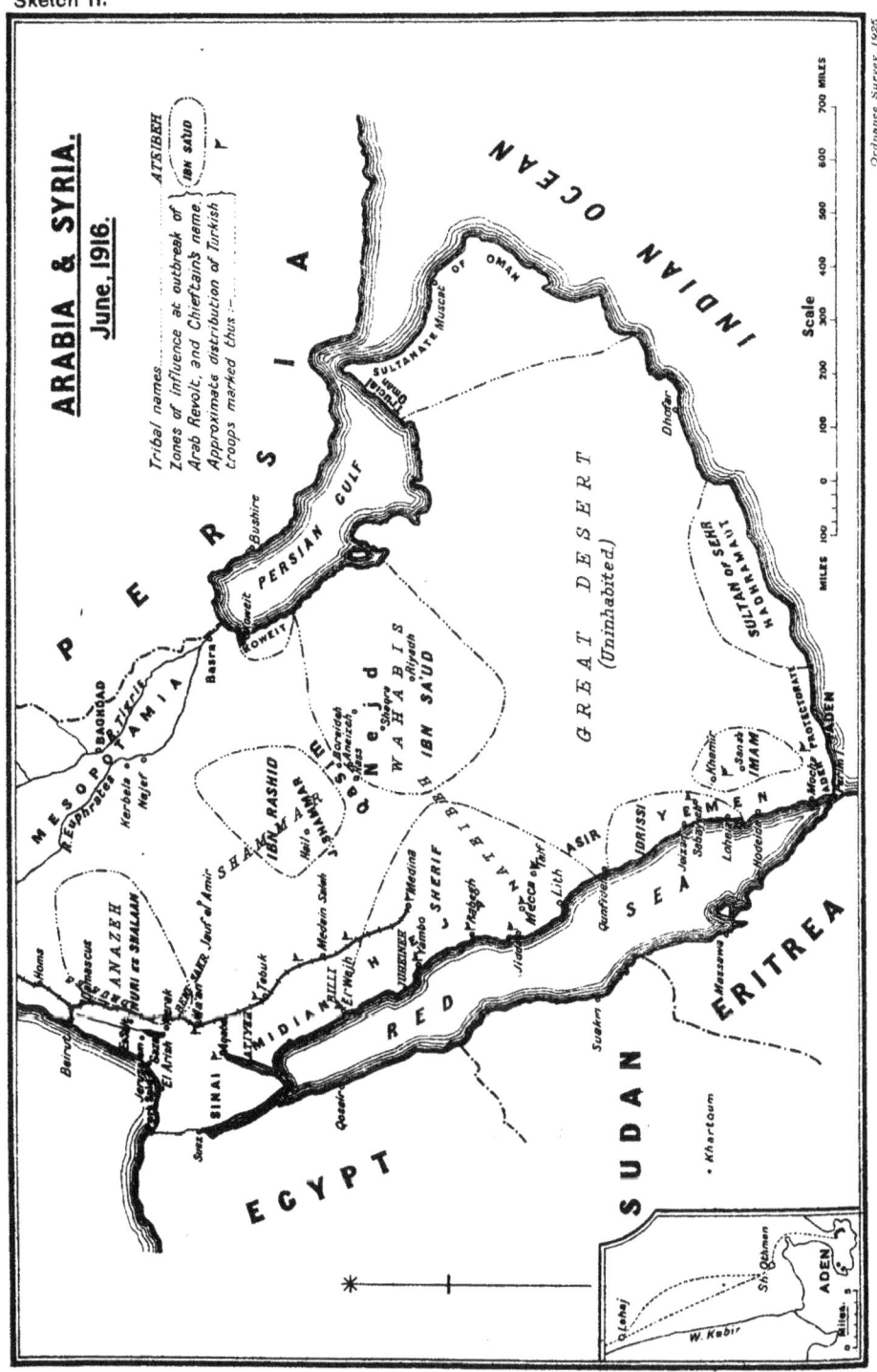

Sketch 12.

Affair of MAGDHABA
Dec.r 23rd 1916

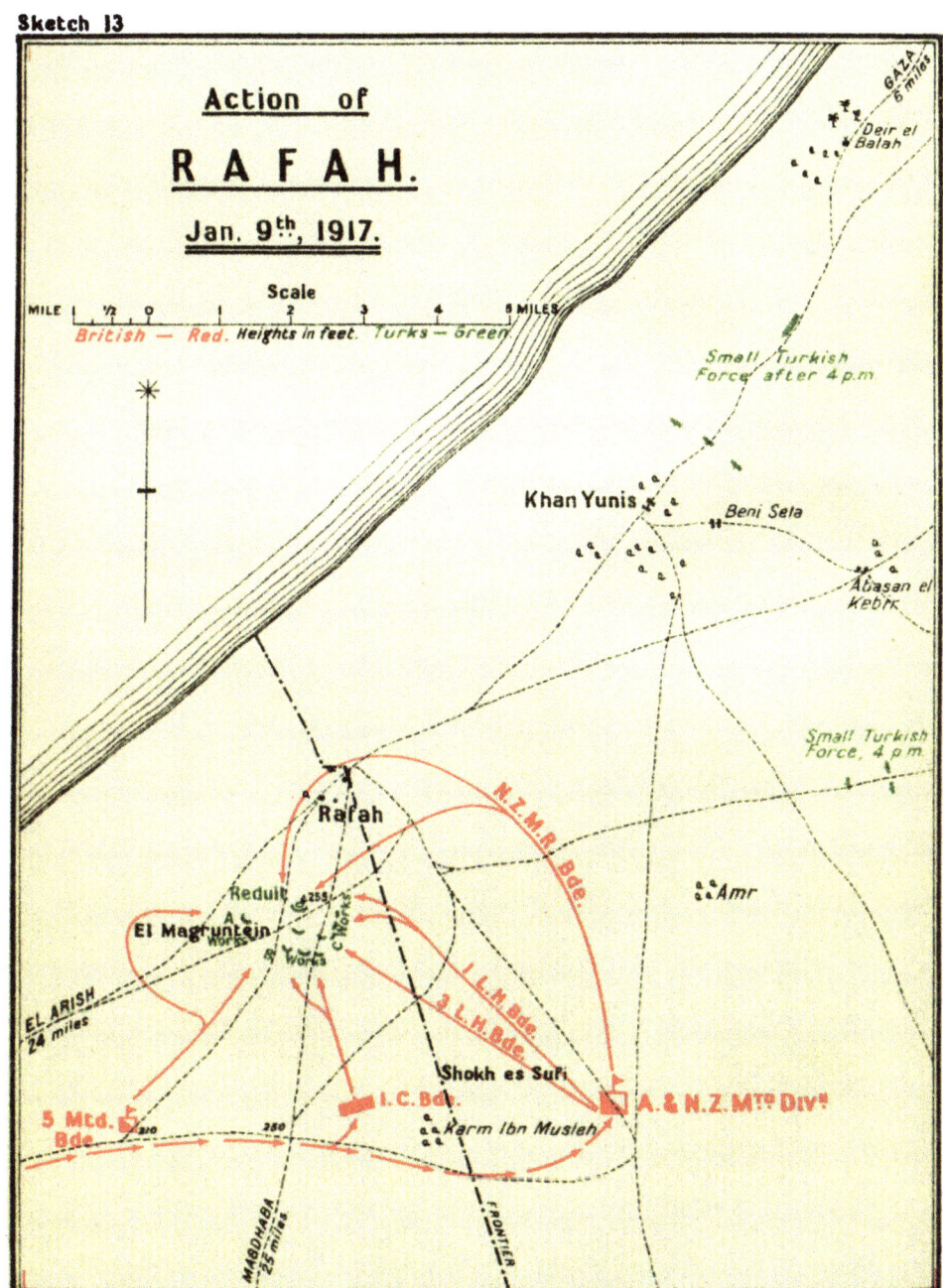

Sketch 14.

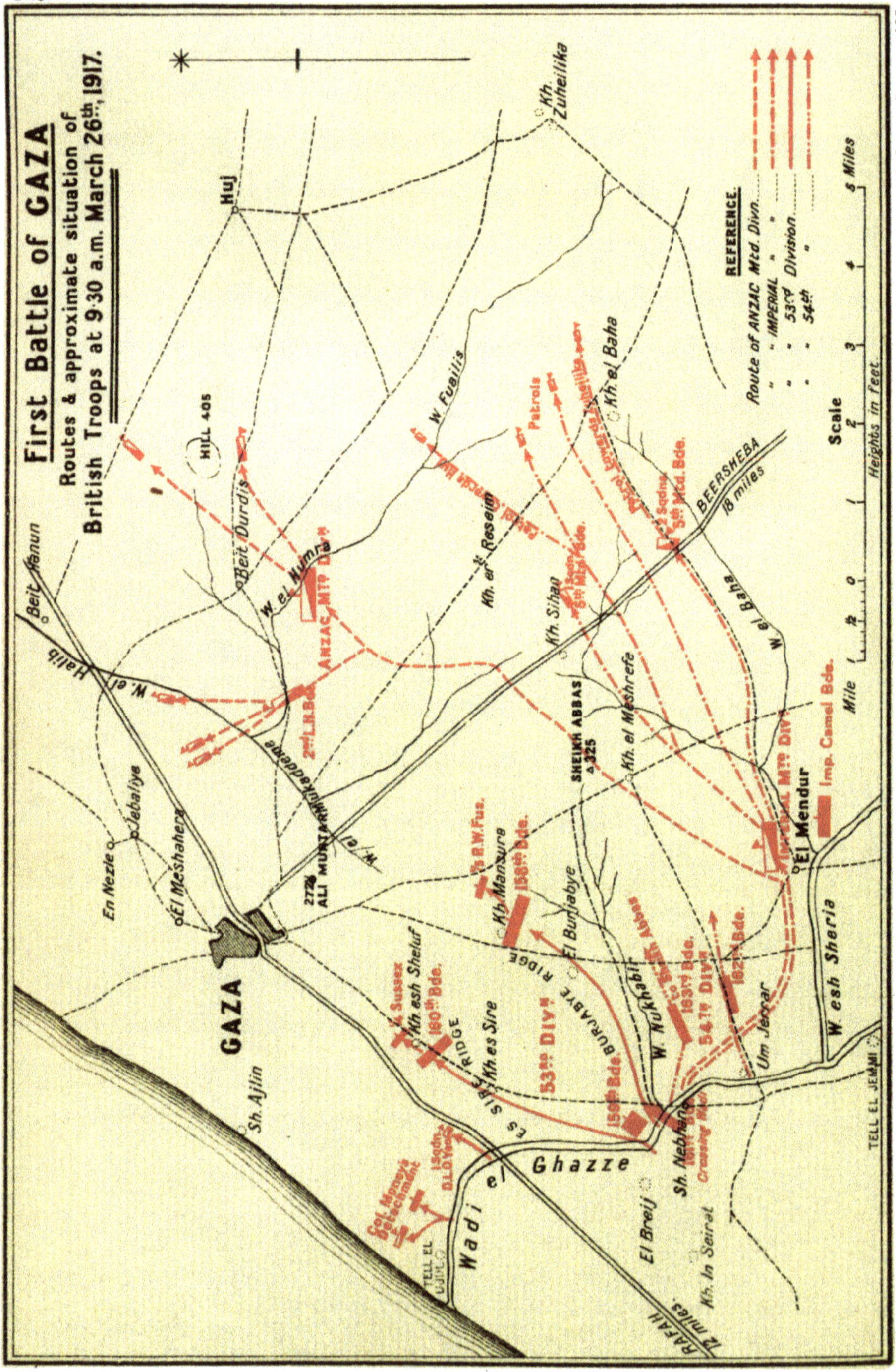

Ordnance Survey, 1925.

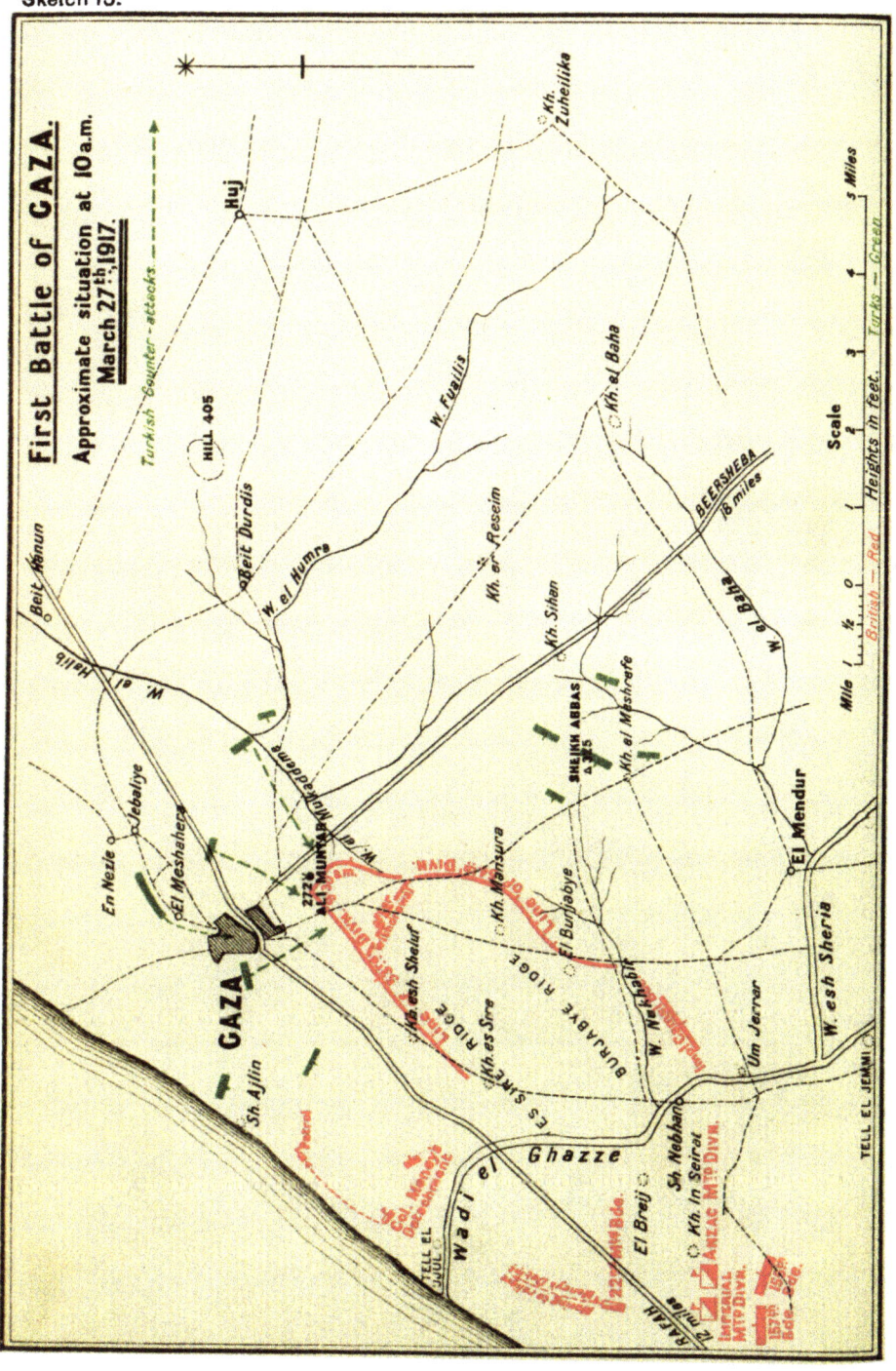

Sketch 16

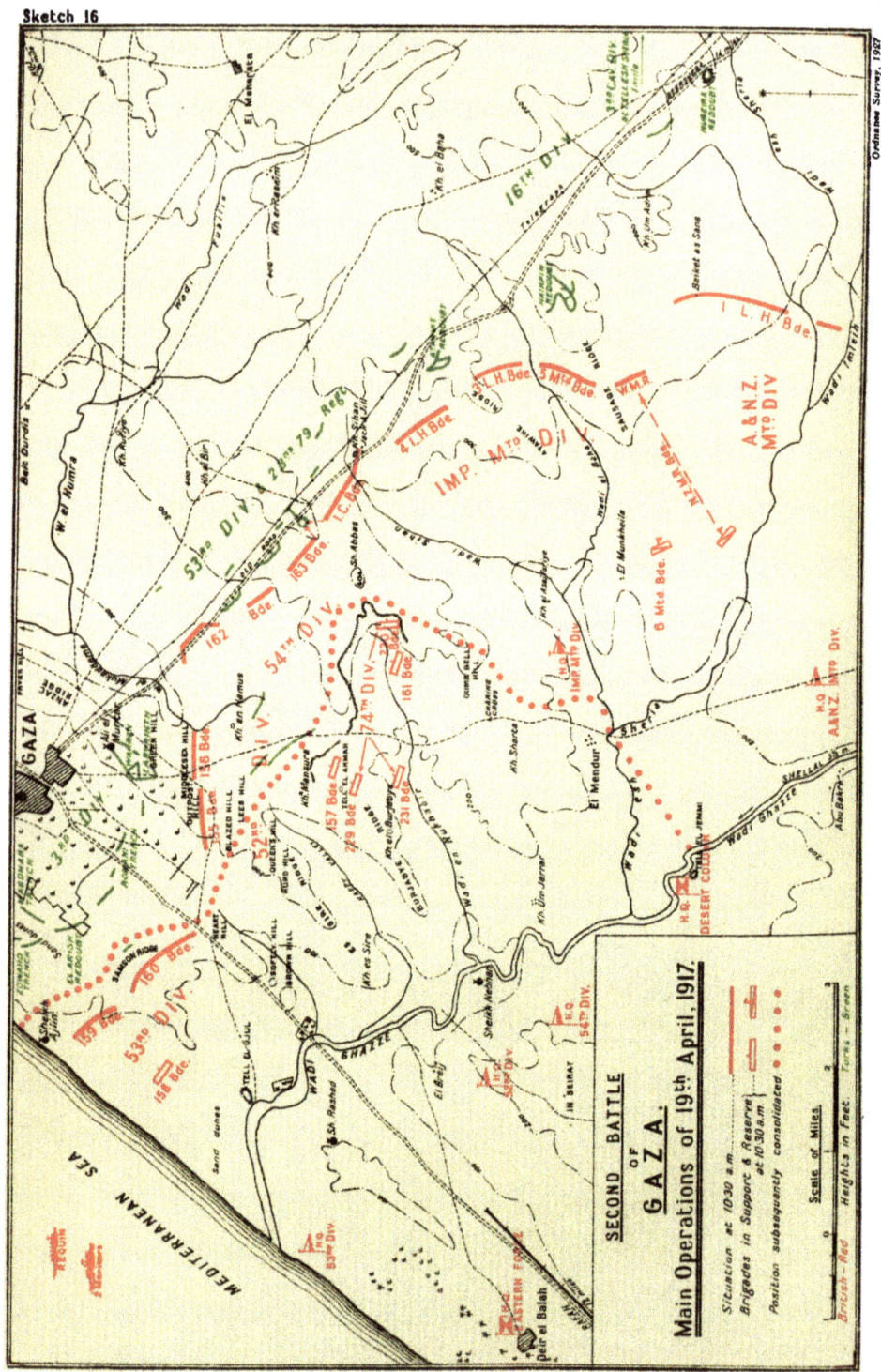

Diagram 1.

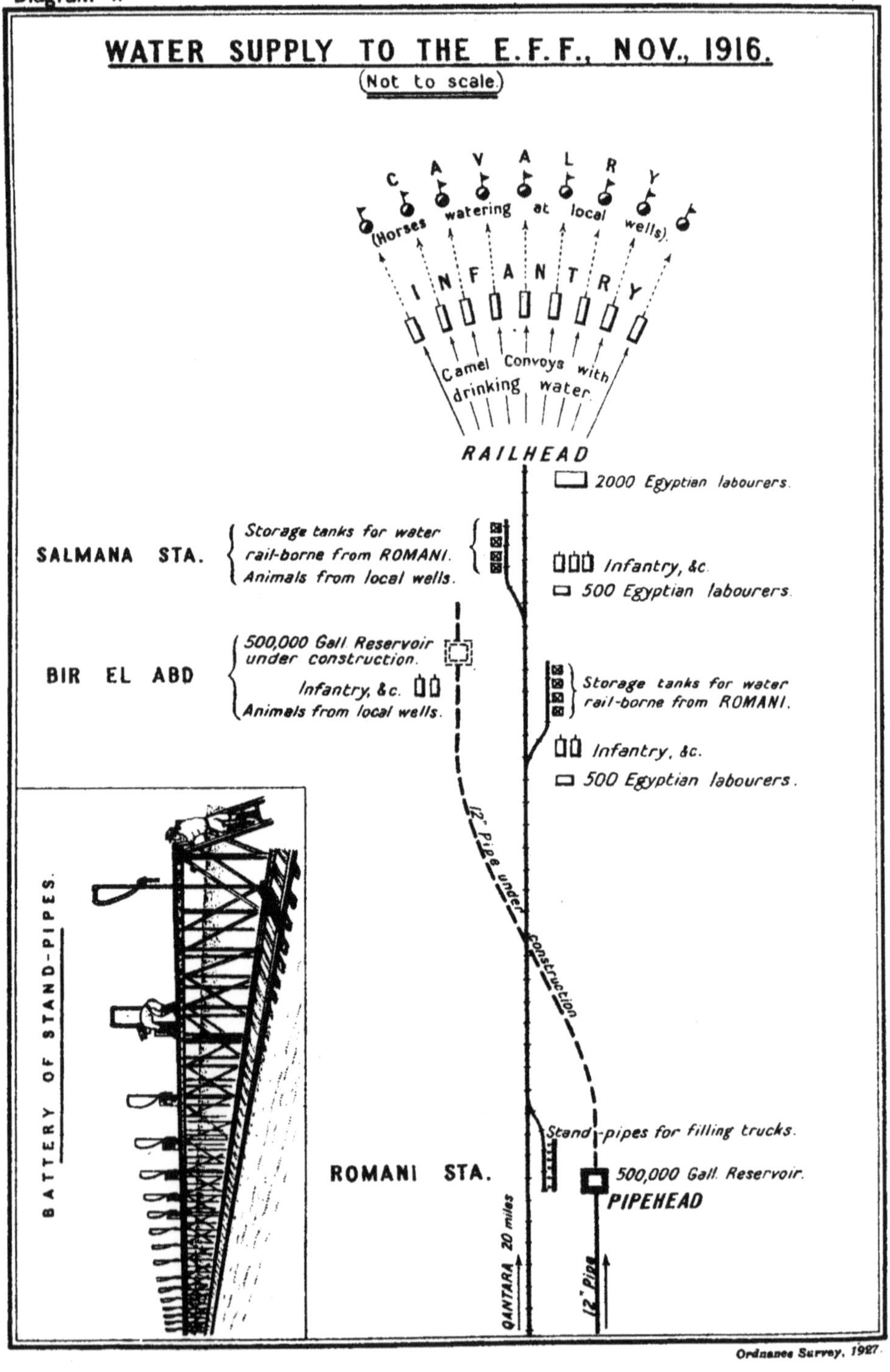

WATER SUPPLY TO THE E.F.F., NOV., 1916.
(Not to scale.)

C A V A L R Y
(Horses watering at local wells)

I N F A N T R Y

Camel Convoys with drinking water

RAILHEAD

2000 Egyptian labourers.

SALMANA STA. { Storage tanks for water rail-borne from ROMANI. Animals from local wells. }

Infantry, &c.
500 Egyptian labourers.

BIR EL ABD { 500,000 Gall. Reservoir under construction. Infantry, &c. Animals from local wells. }

Storage tanks for water rail-borne from ROMANI.

Infantry, &c.
500 Egyptian labourers.

12" Pipe under construction

BATTERY OF STAND-PIPES.

ROMANI STA.

Stand-pipes for filling trucks.
500,000 Gall. Reservoir.
PIPEHEAD

QANTARA 20 miles
12" Pipe

Ordnance Survey, 1927.

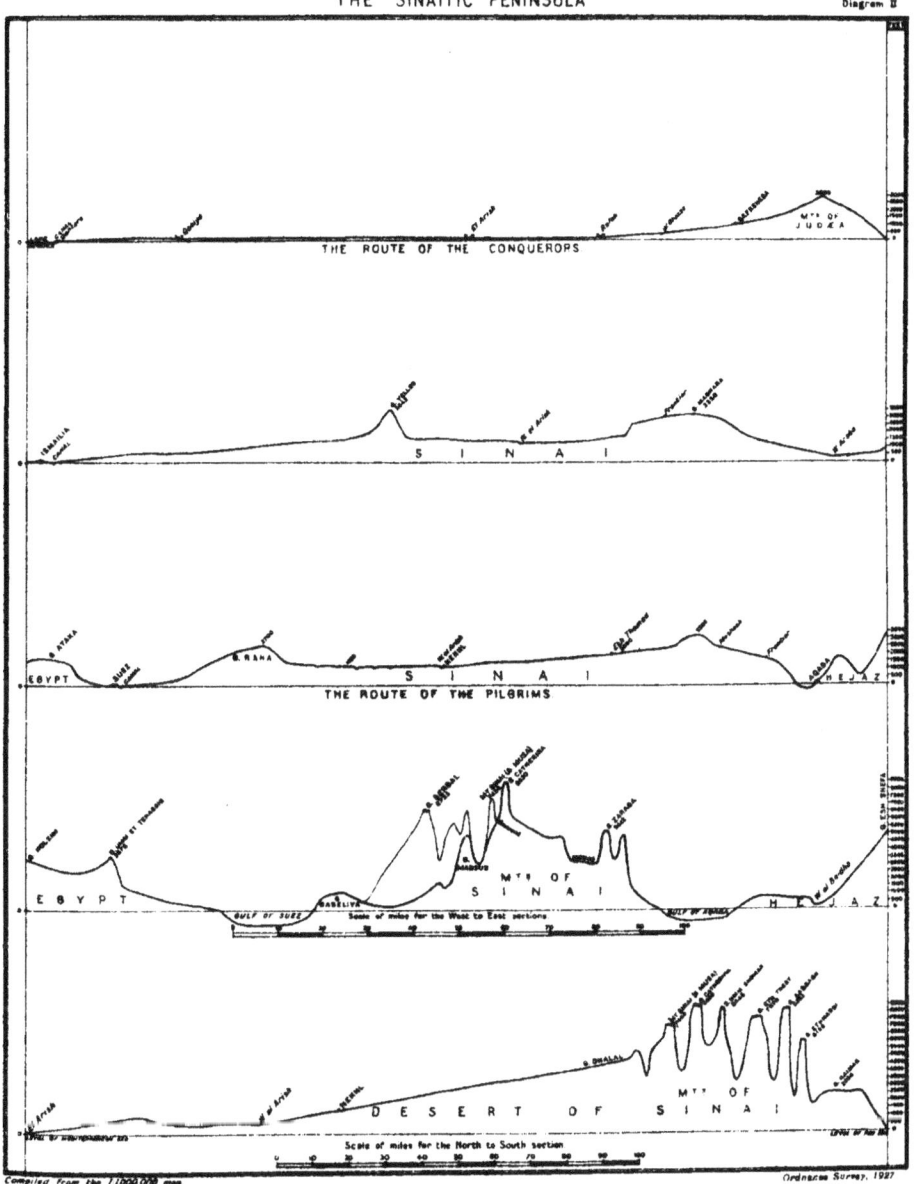

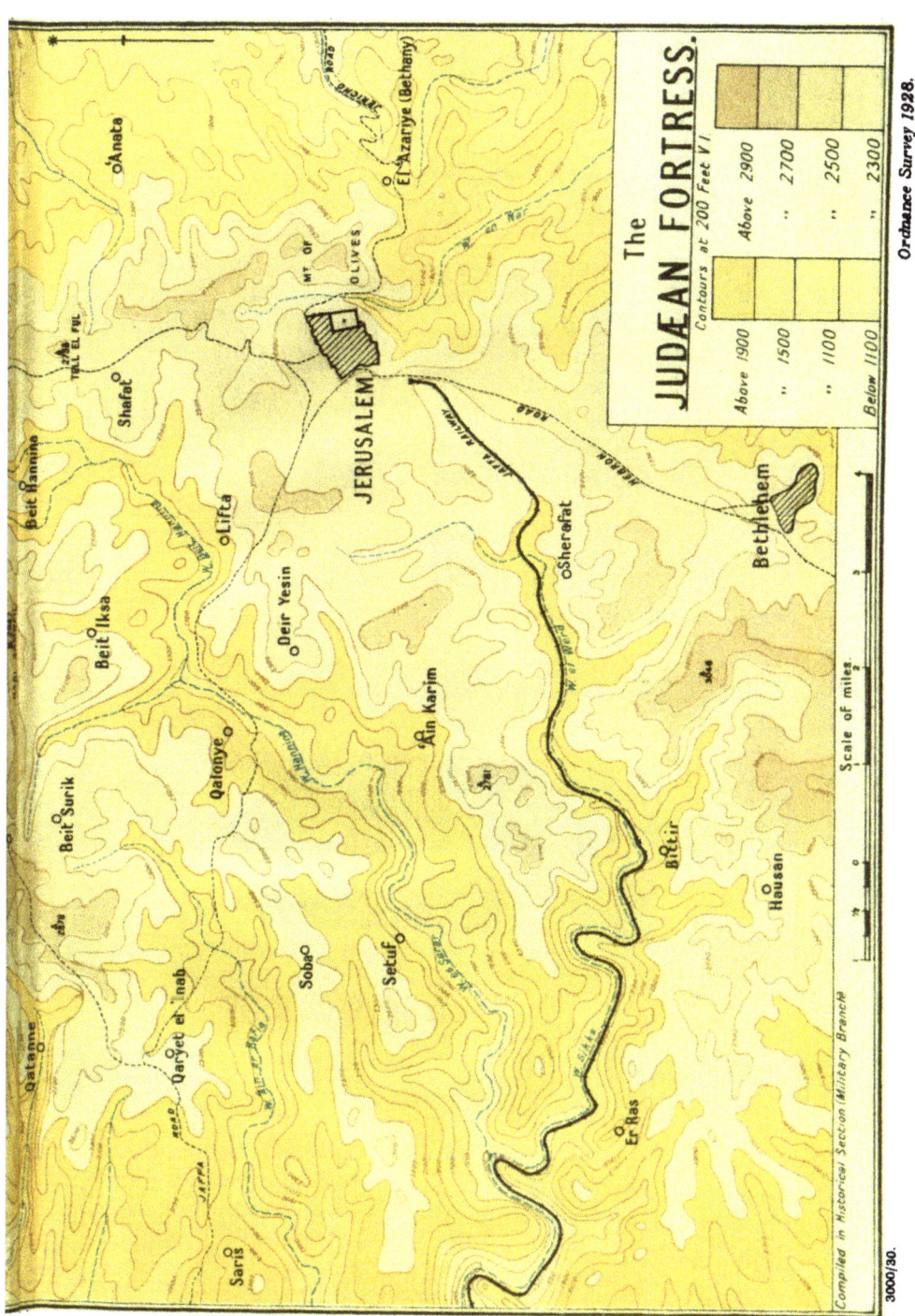

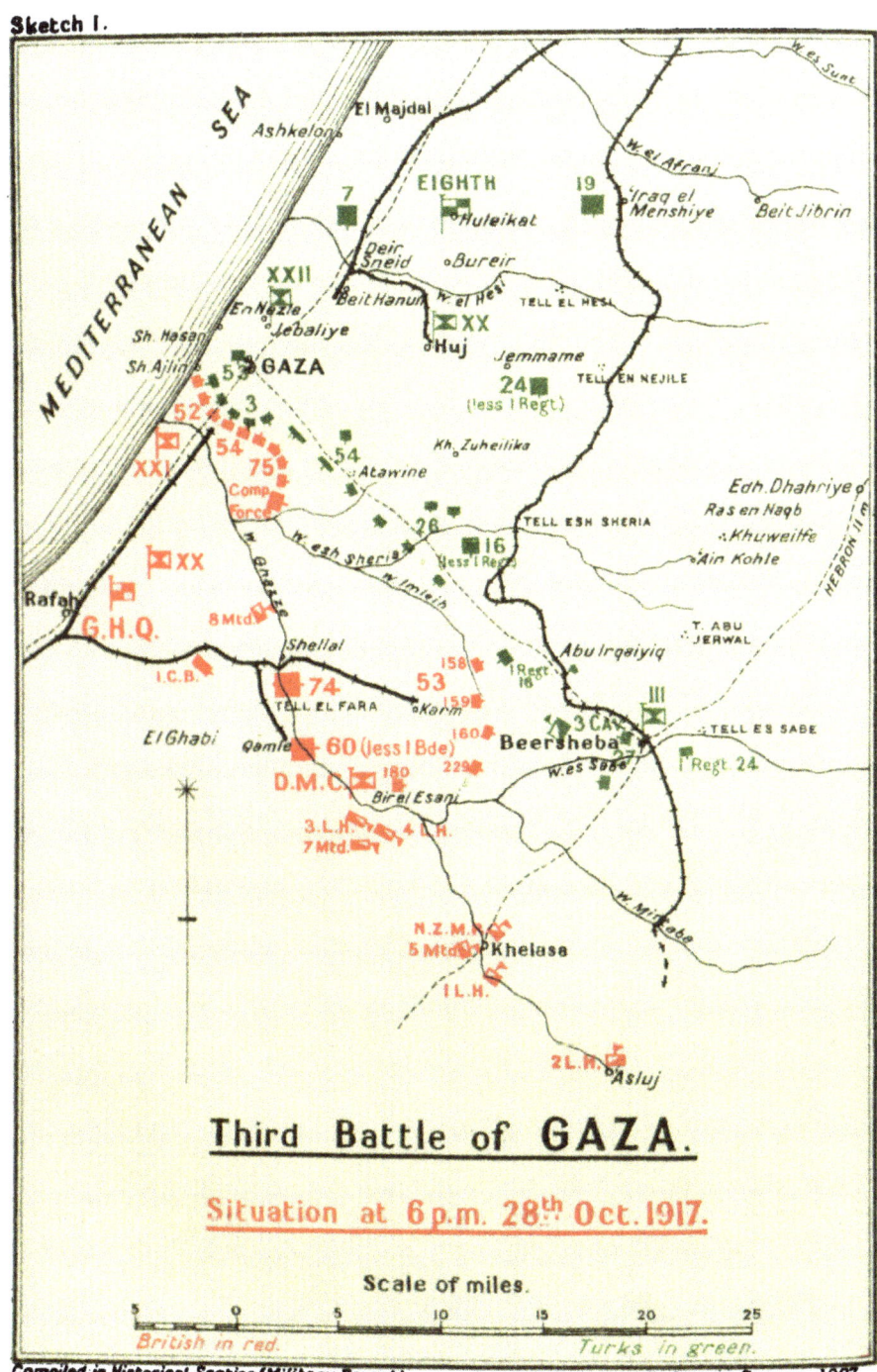

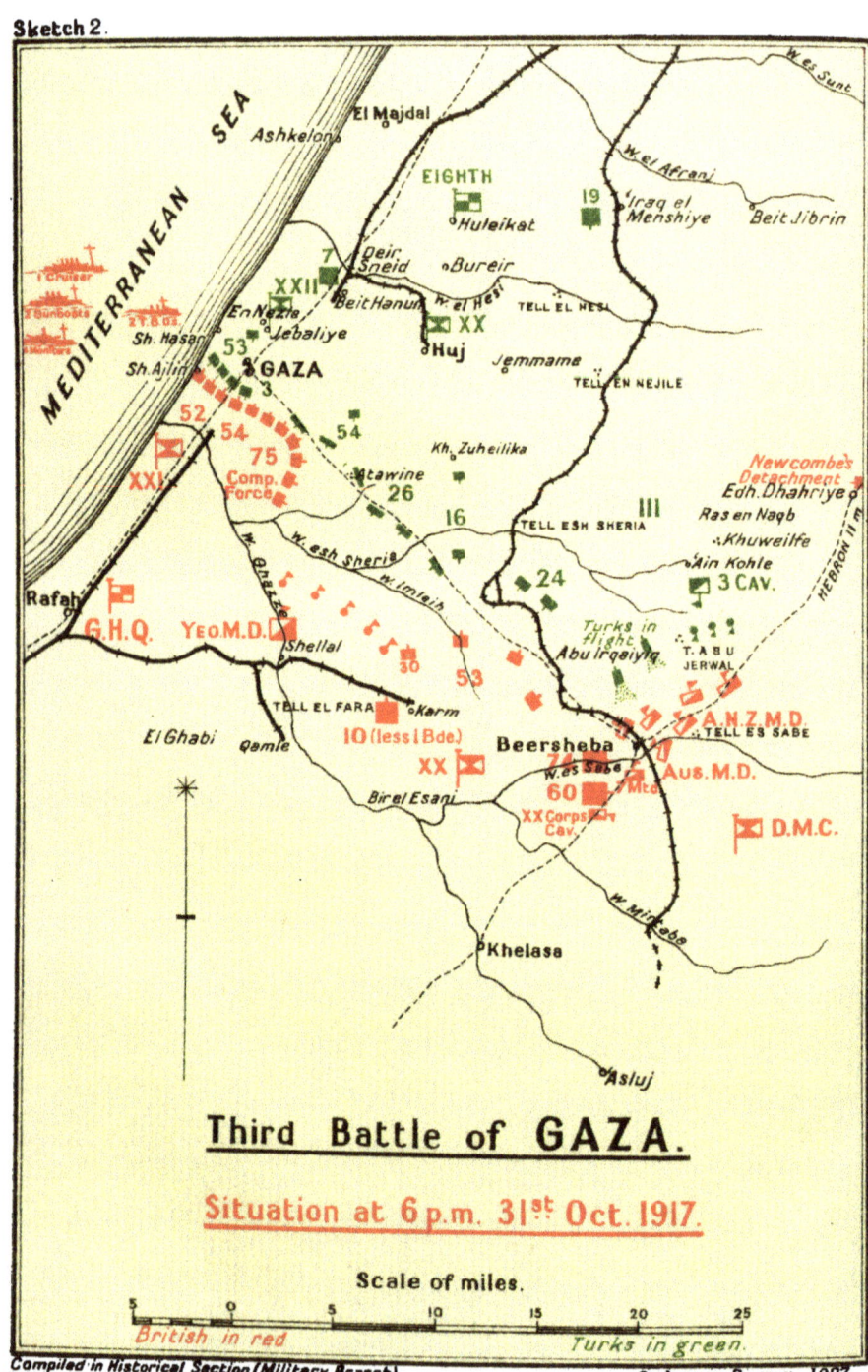

Sketch 3

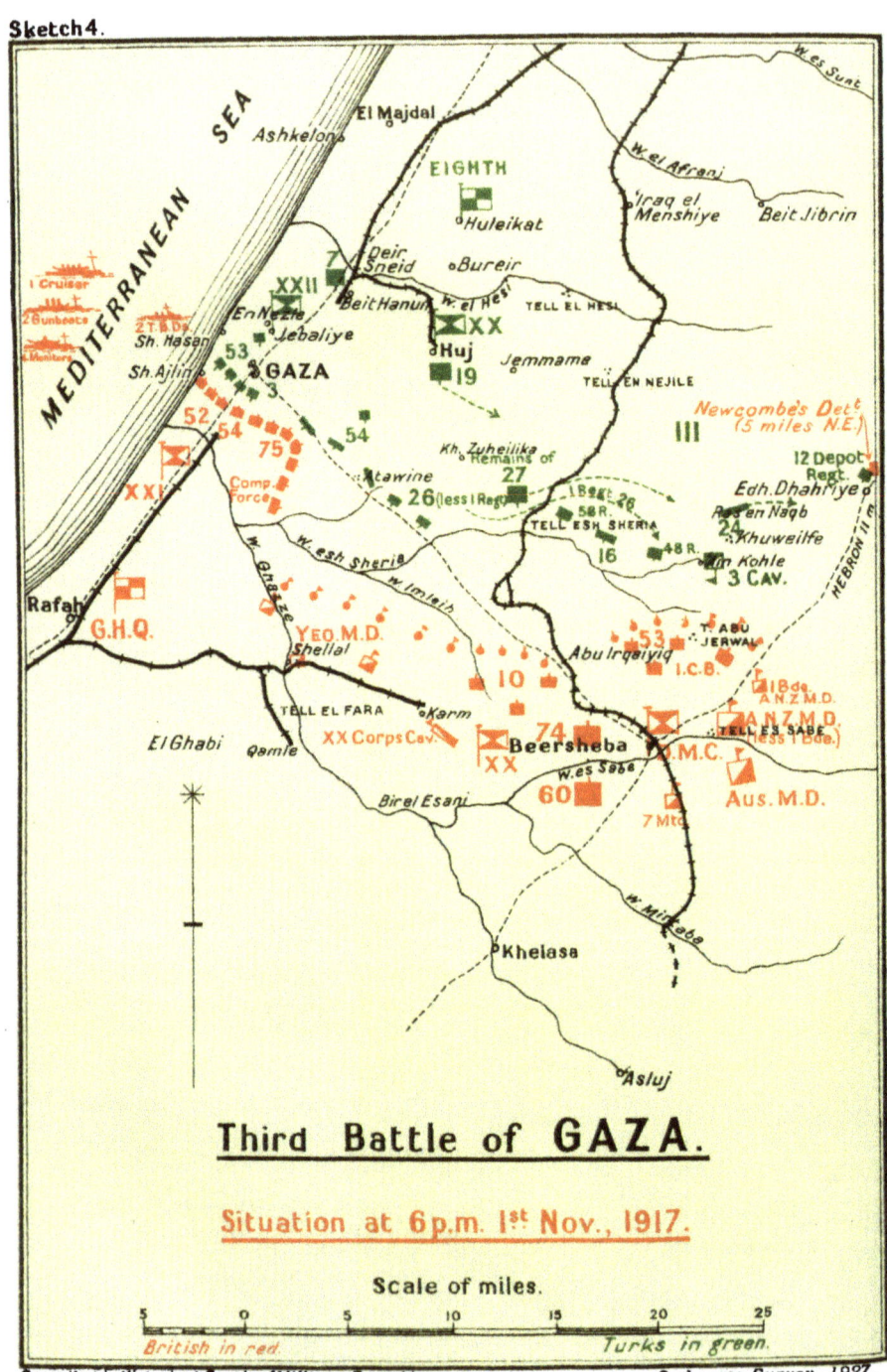

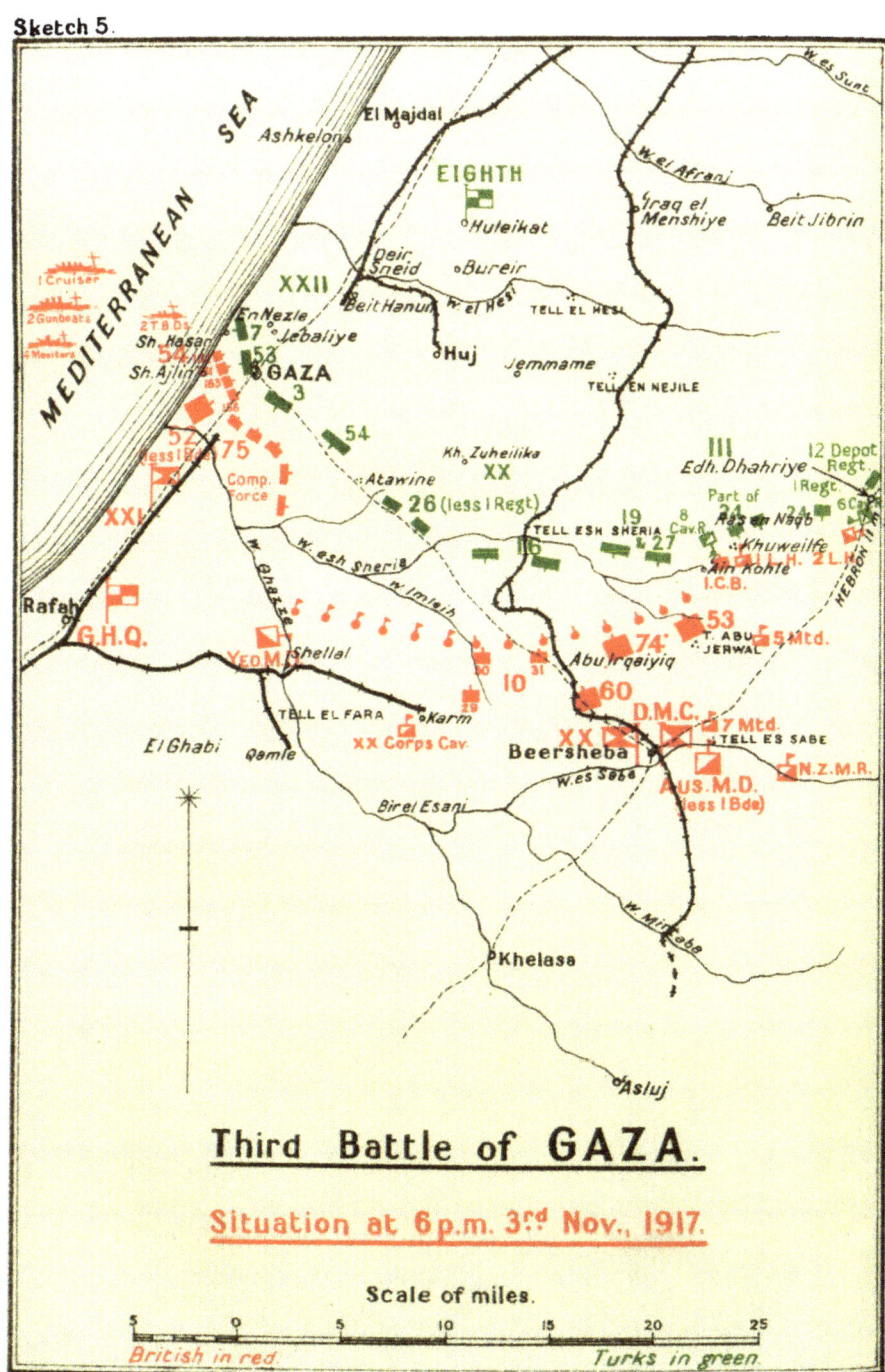

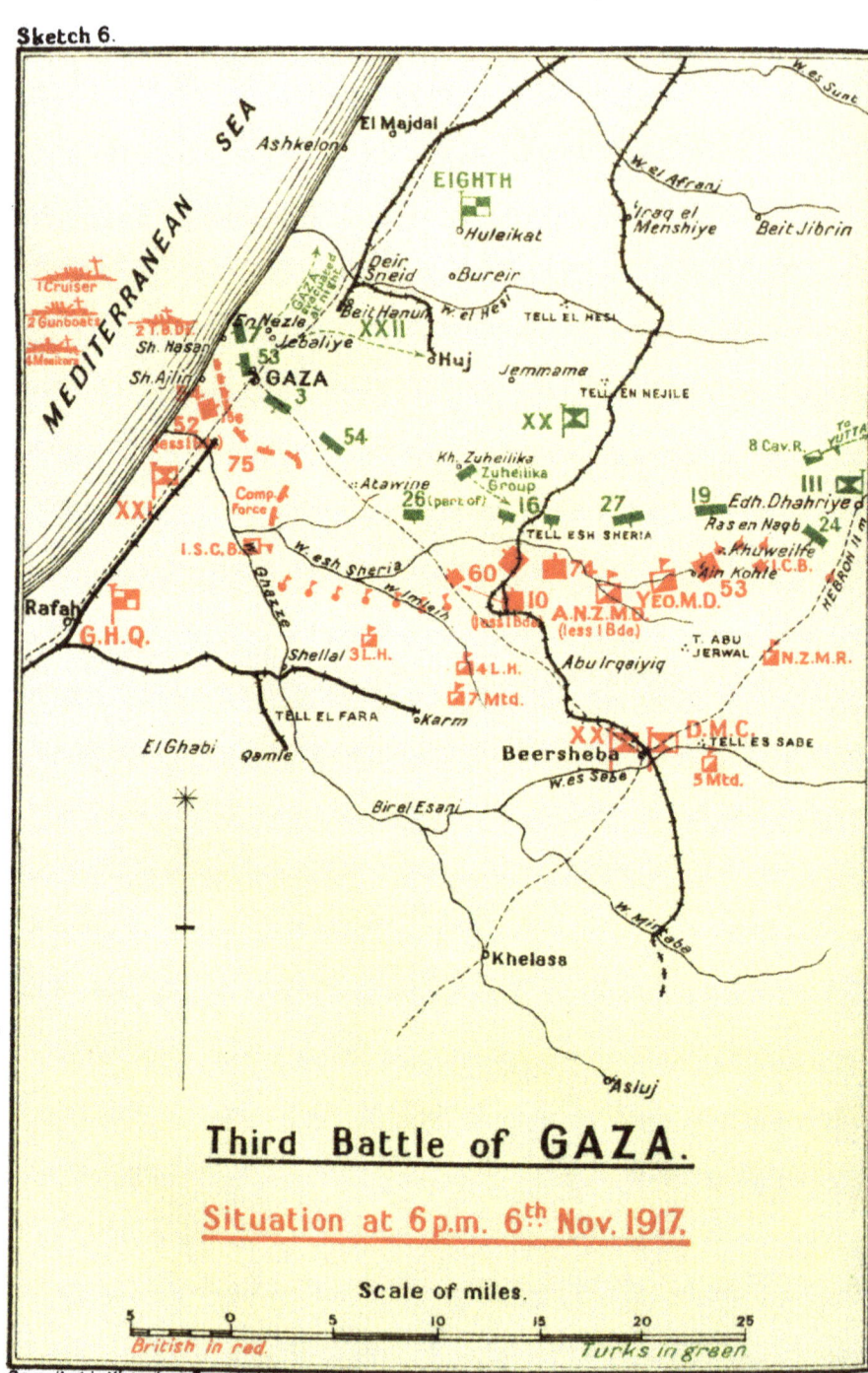

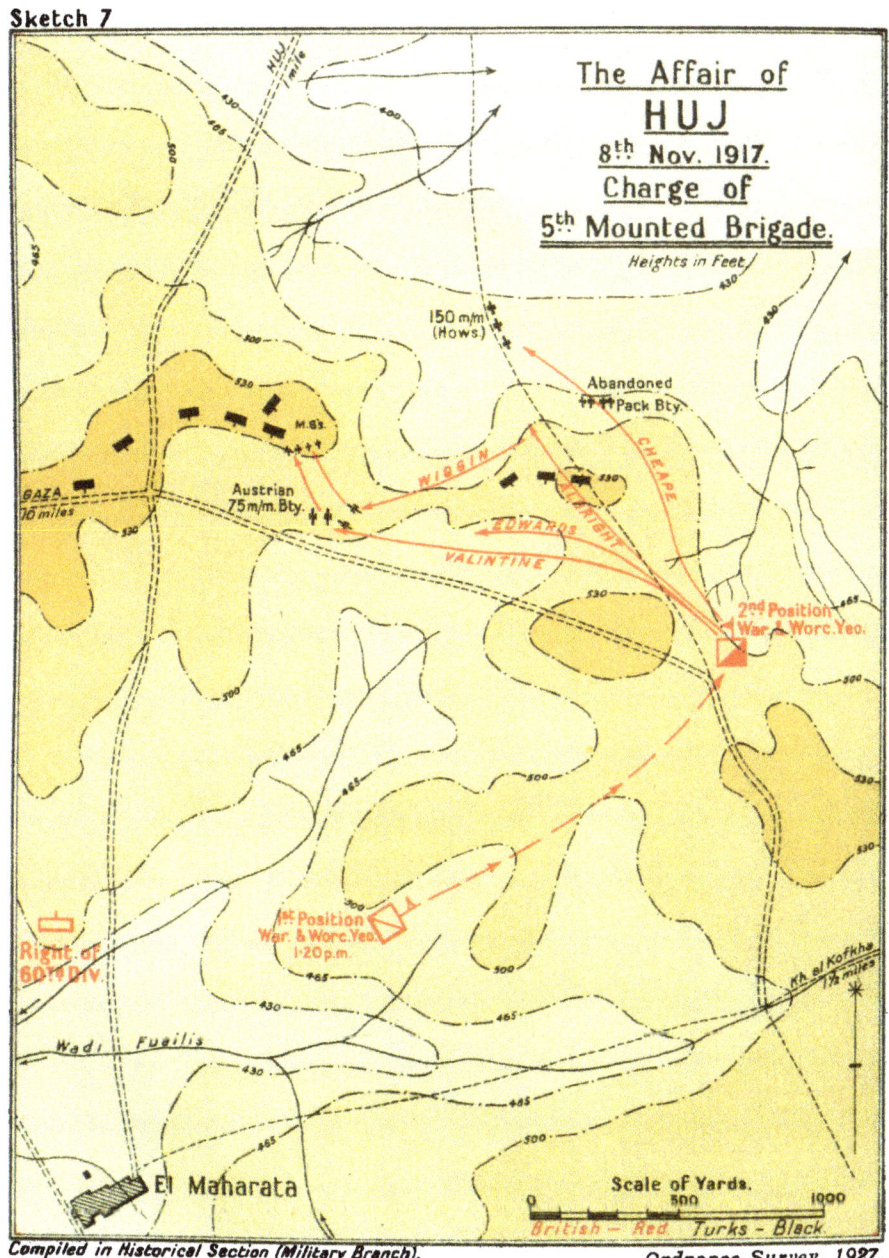

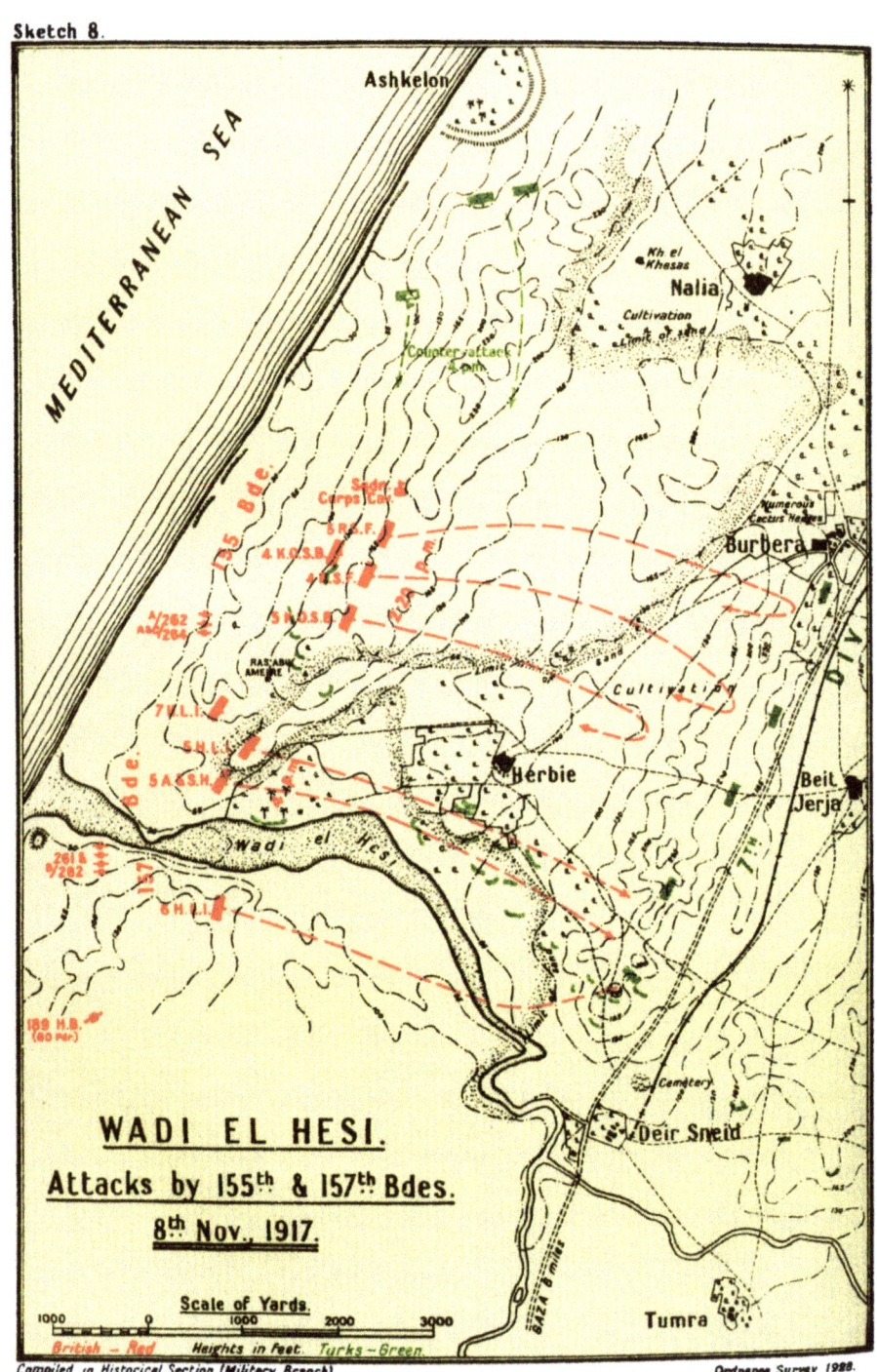

Sketch 9.

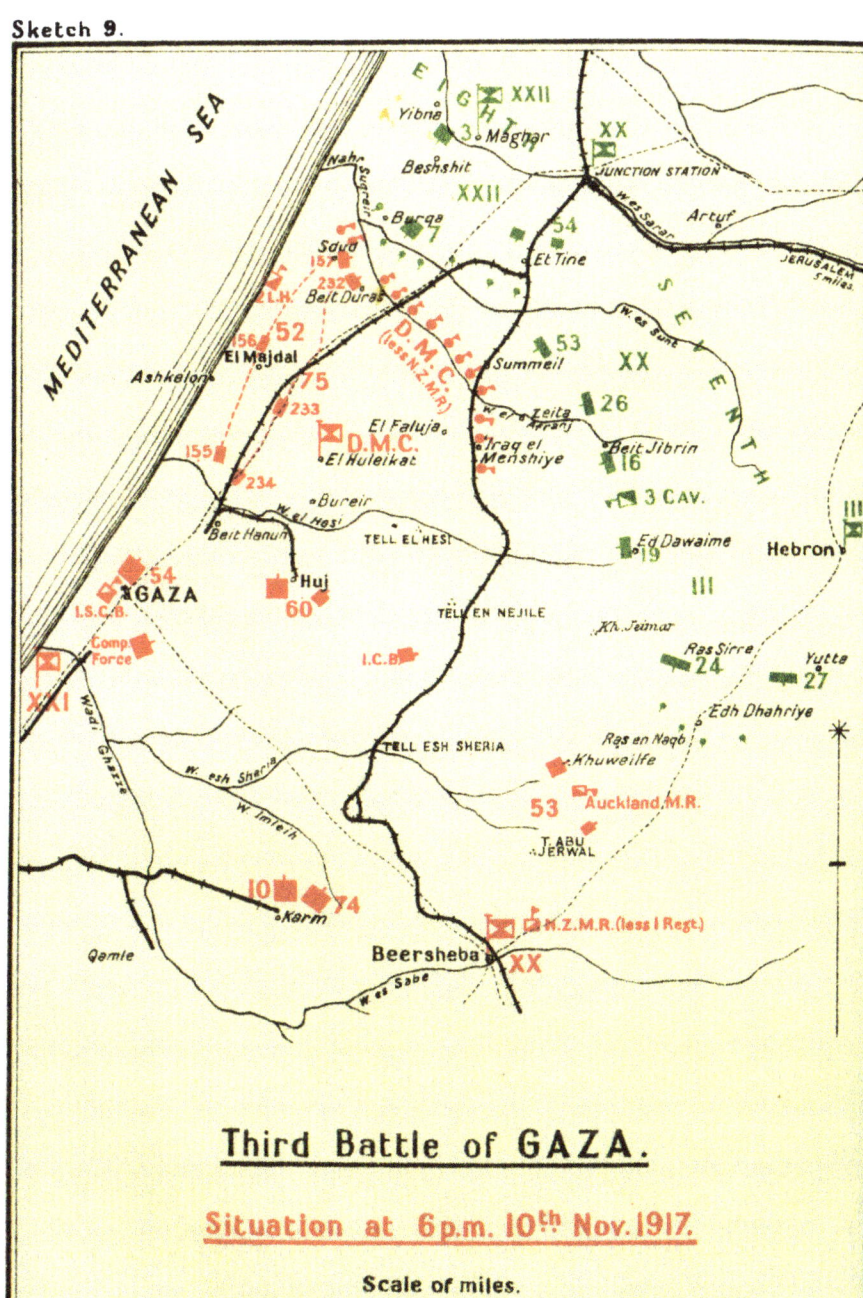

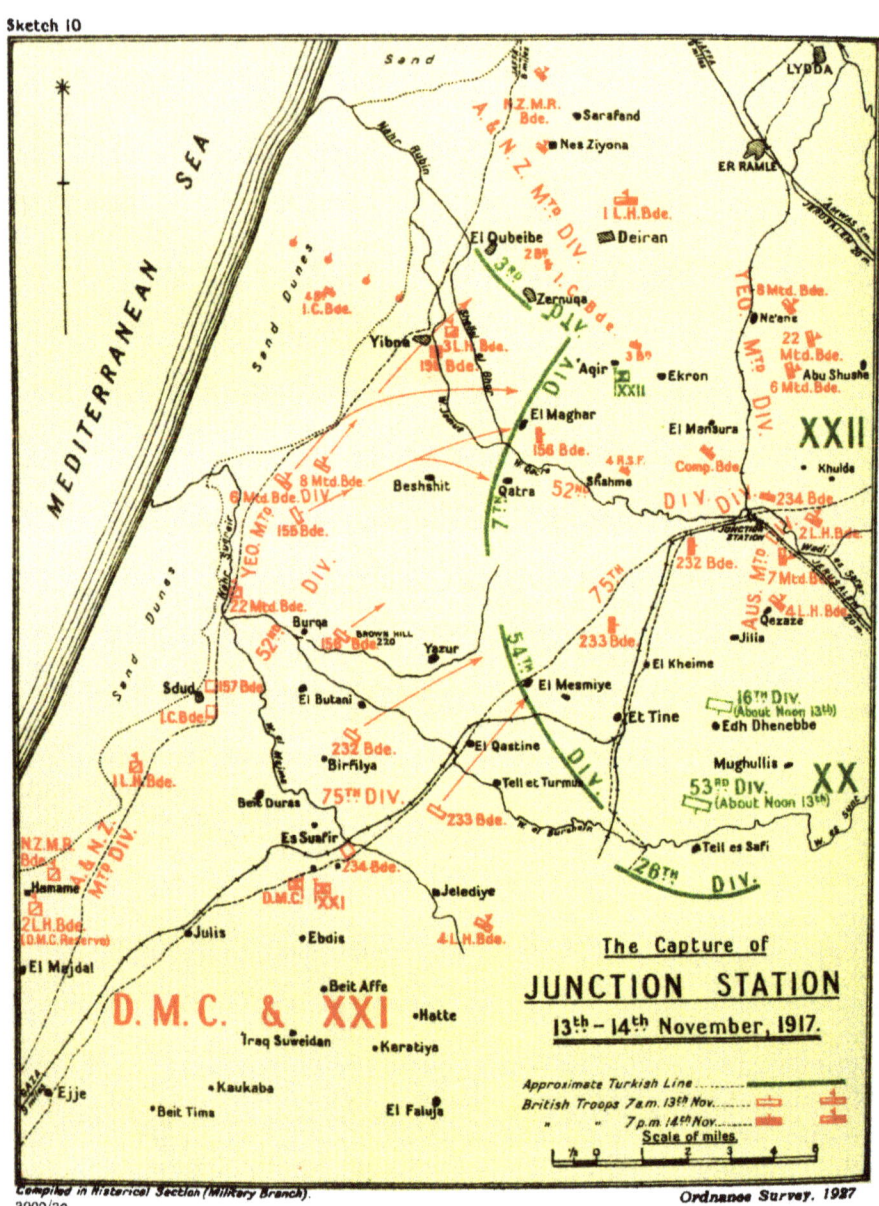

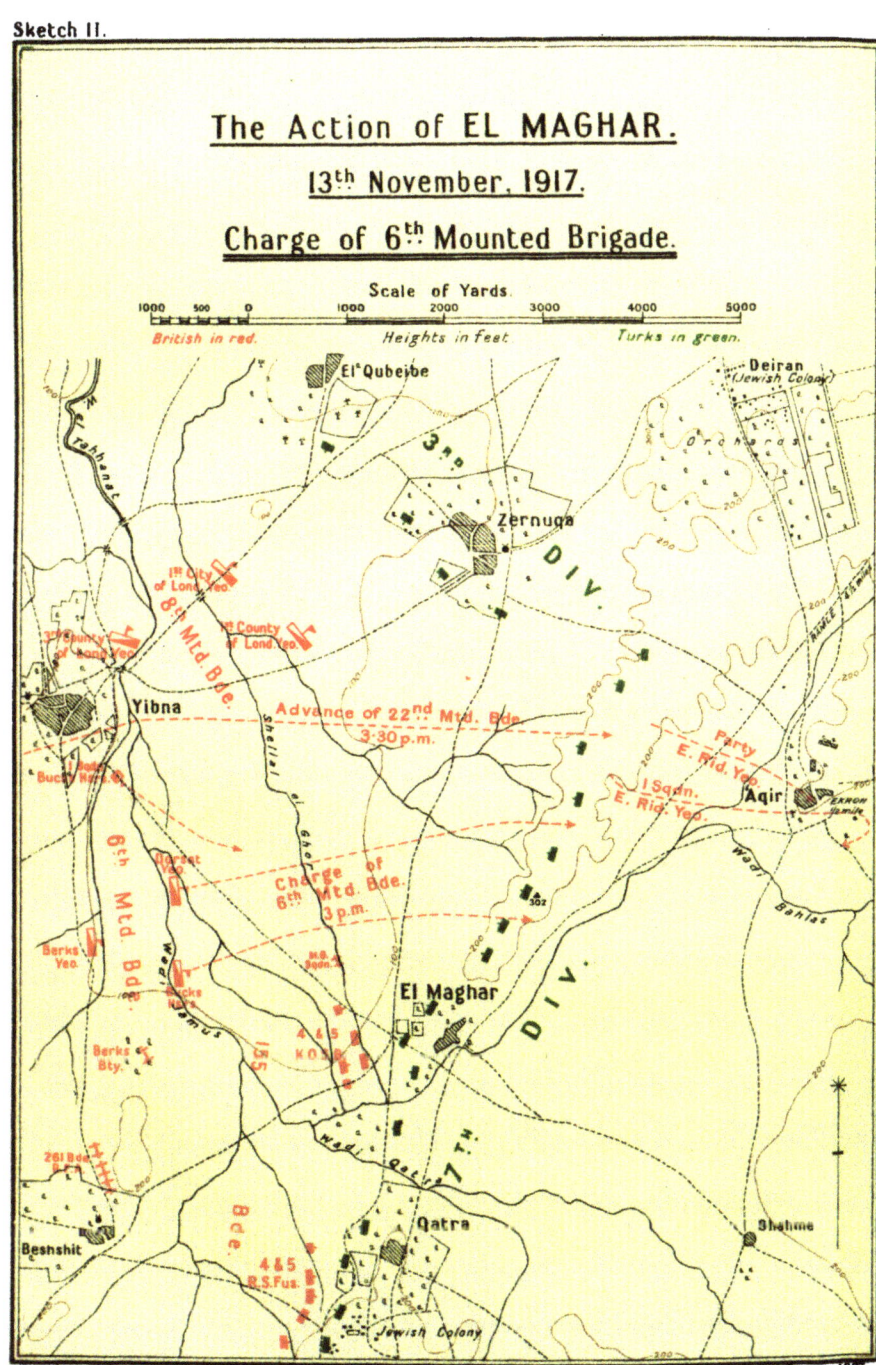

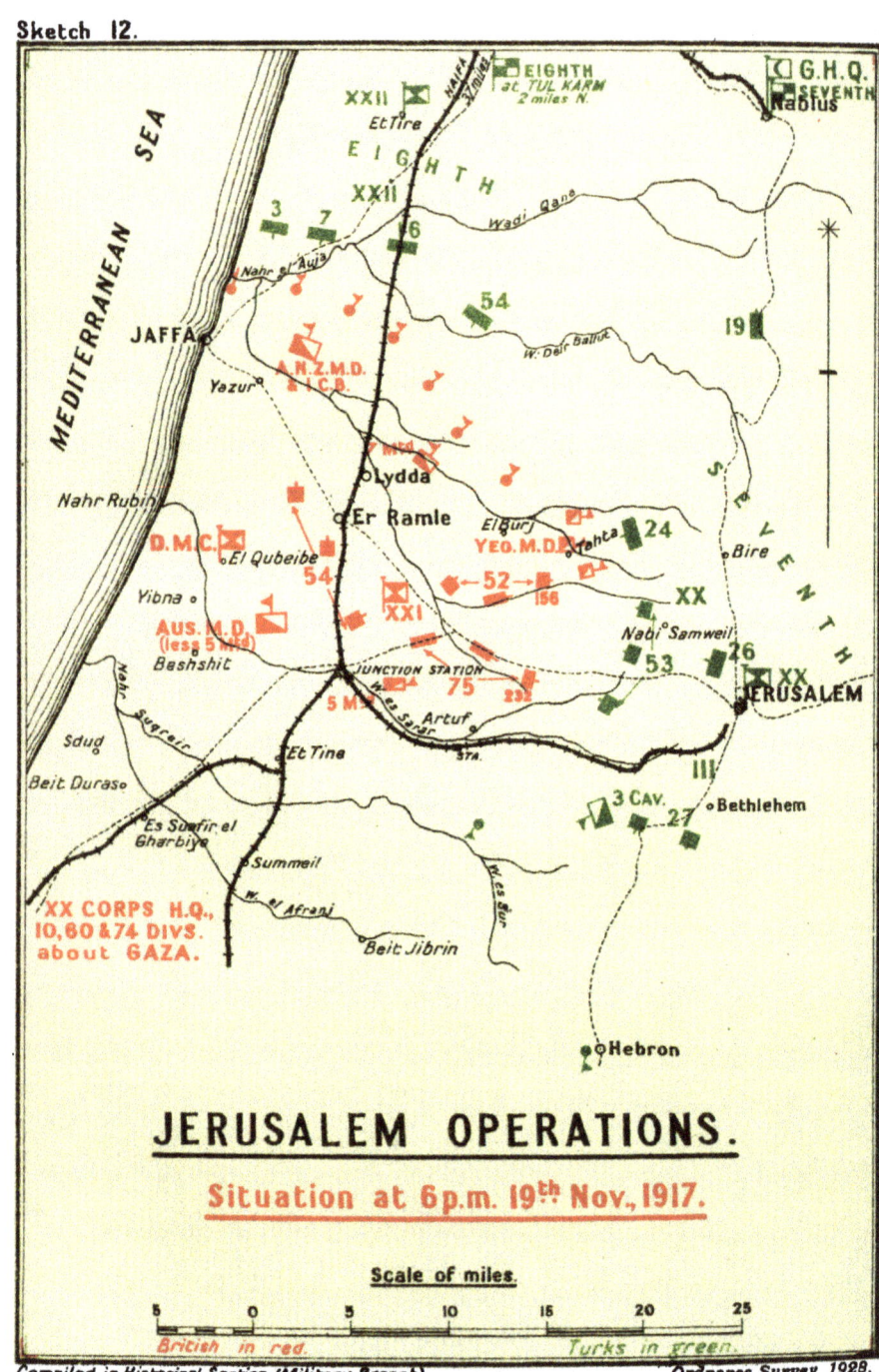

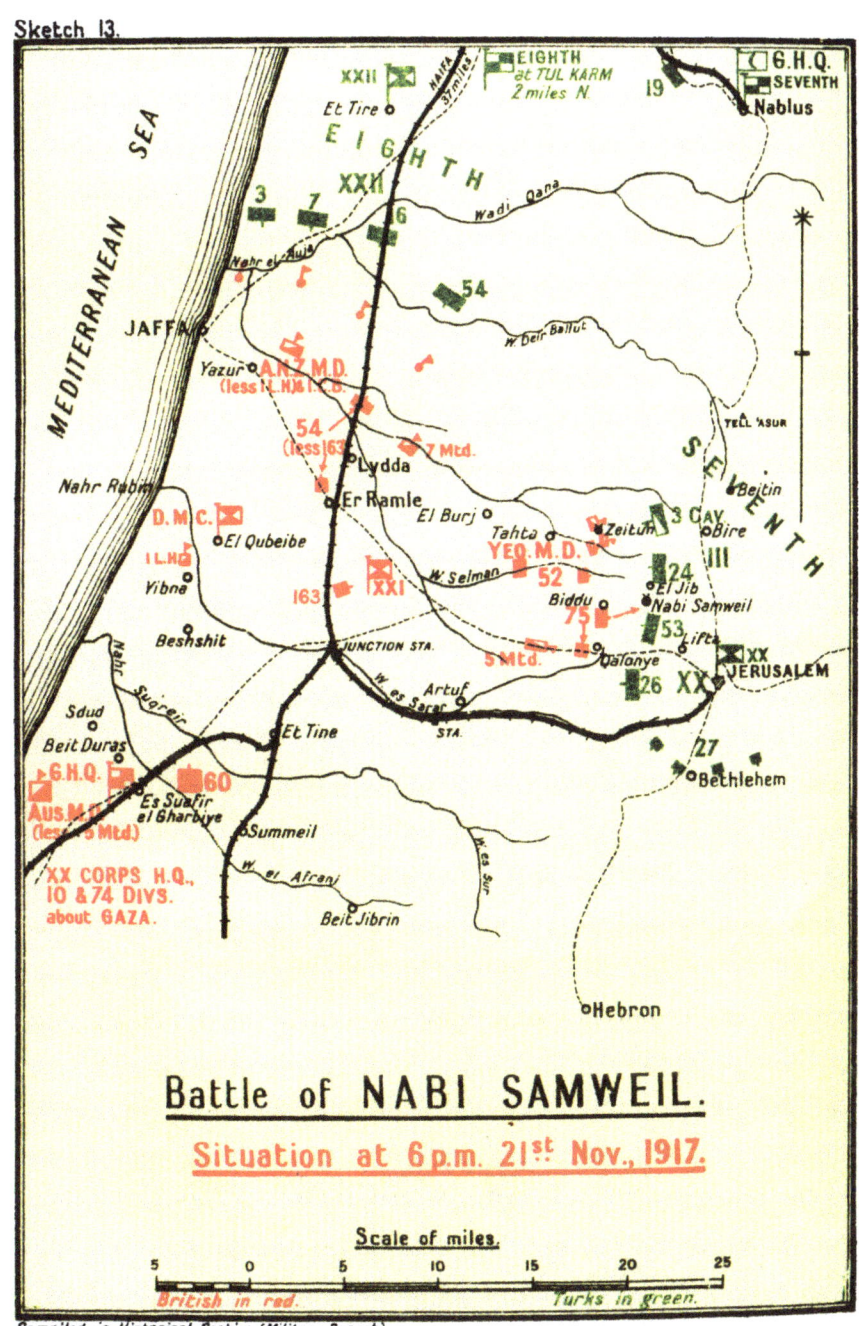

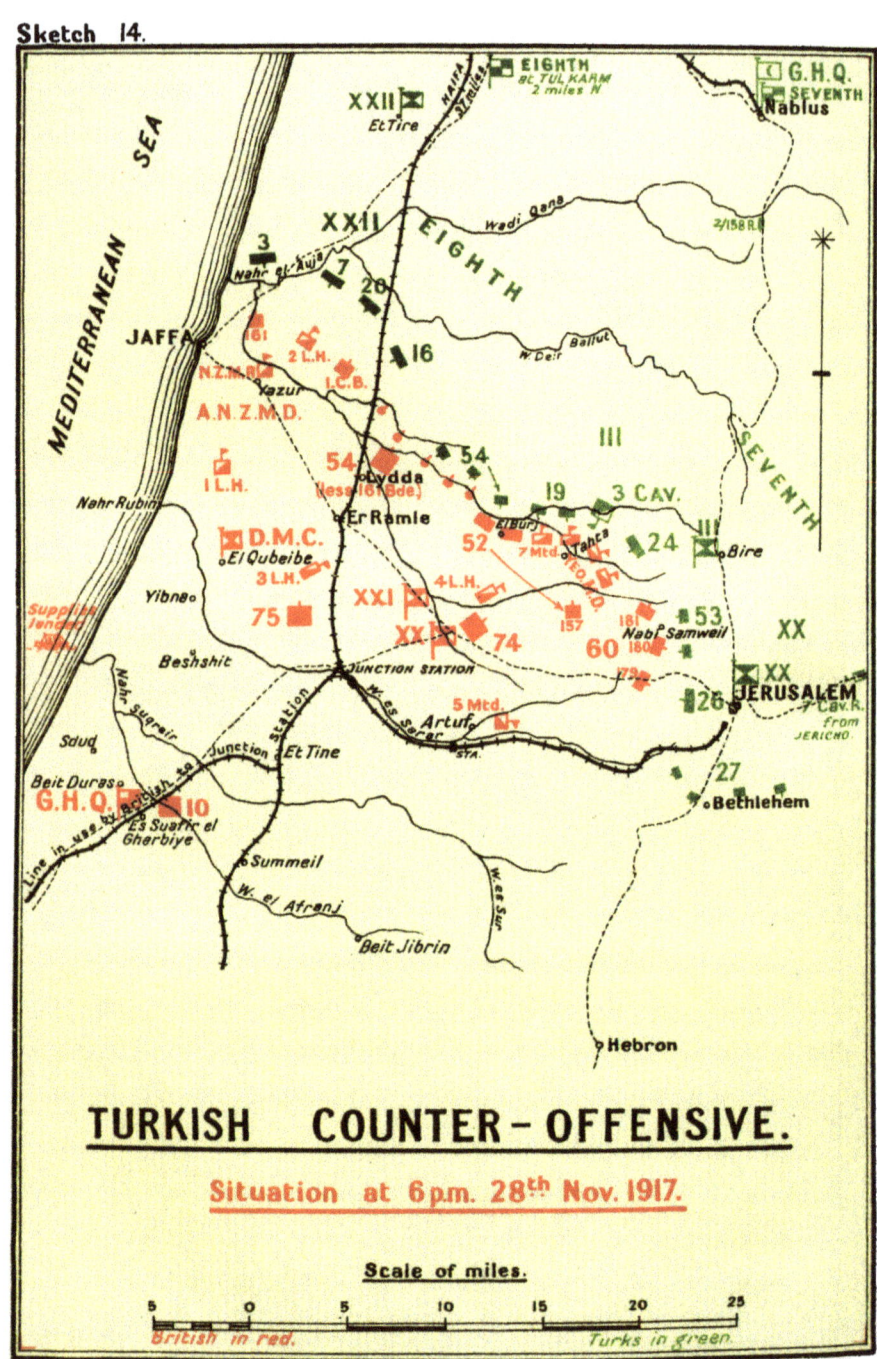

Sketch 15.

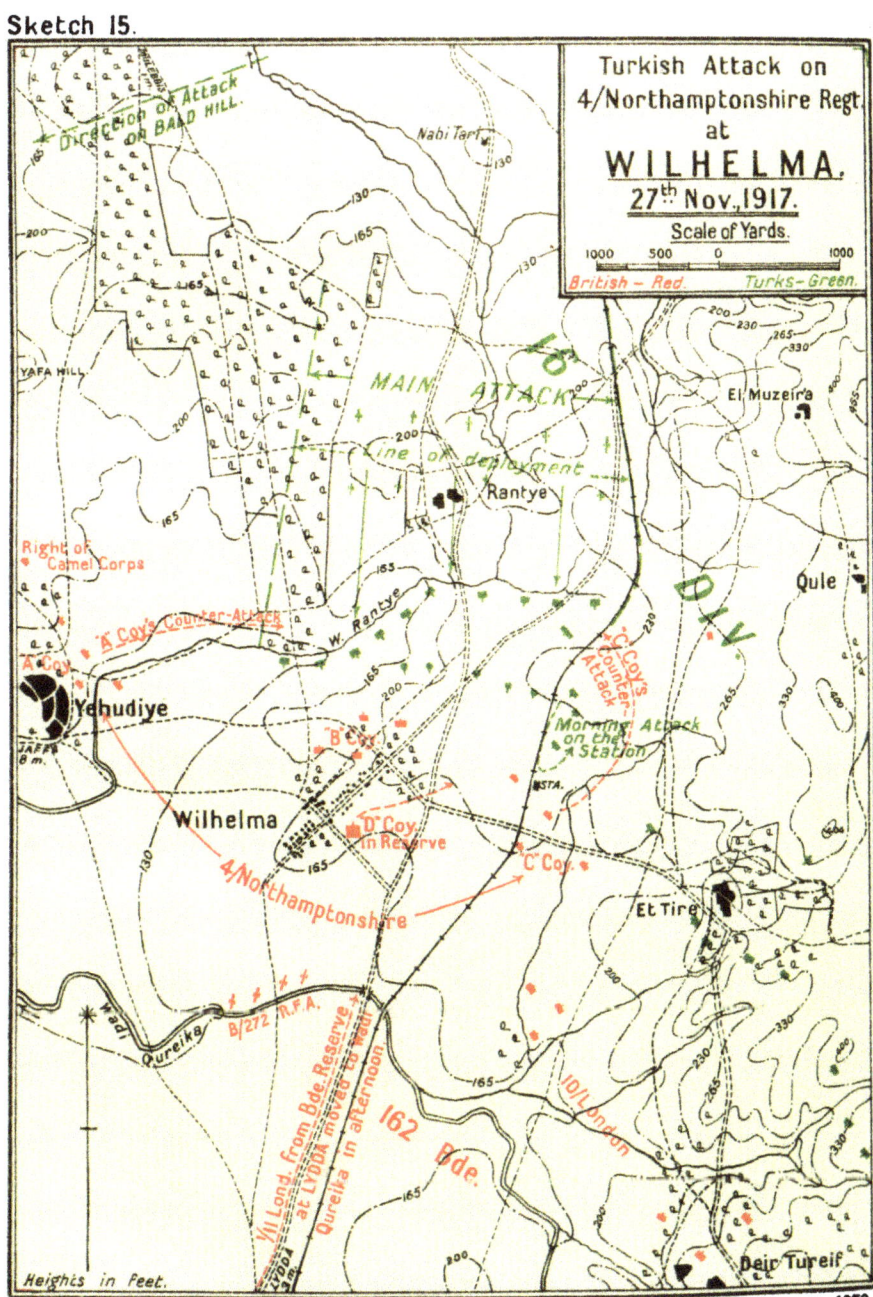

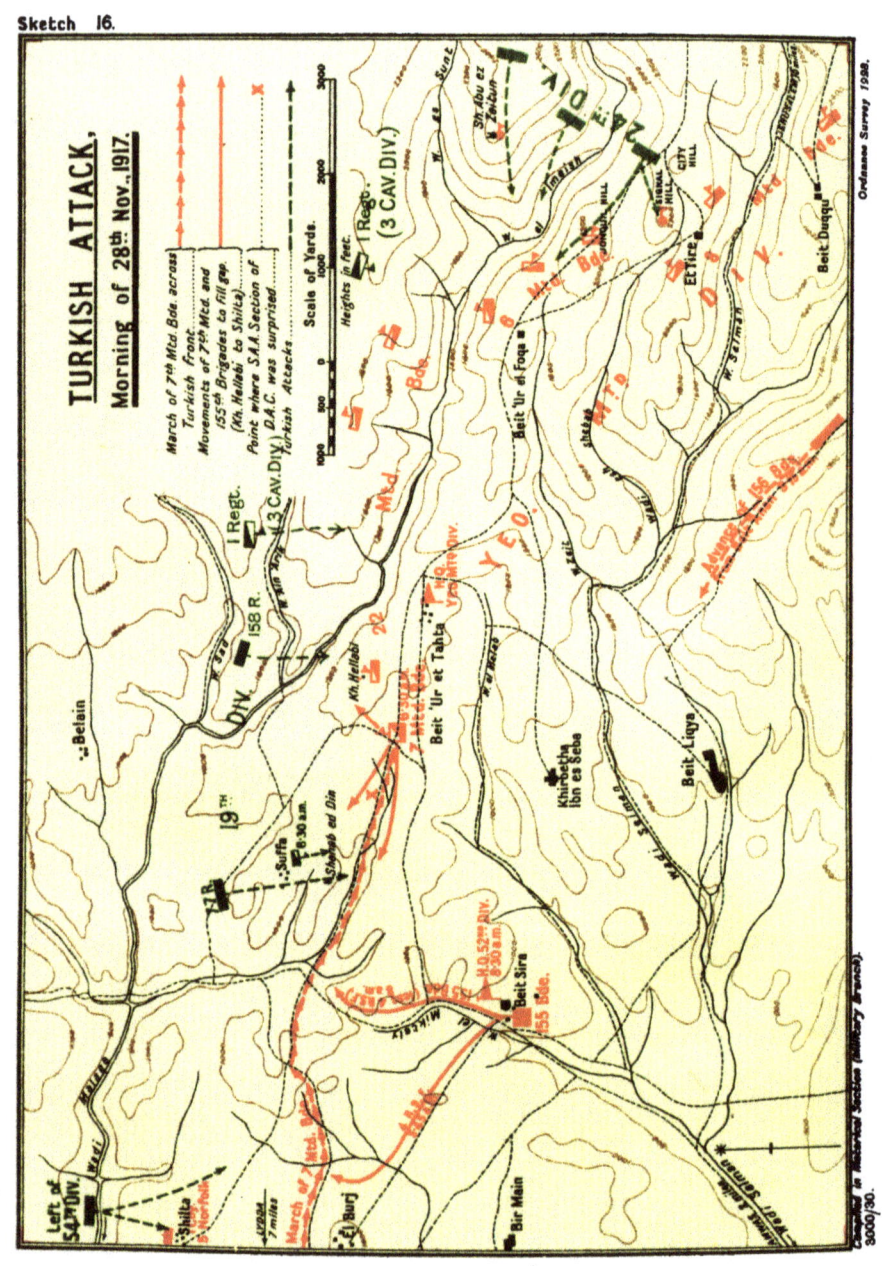

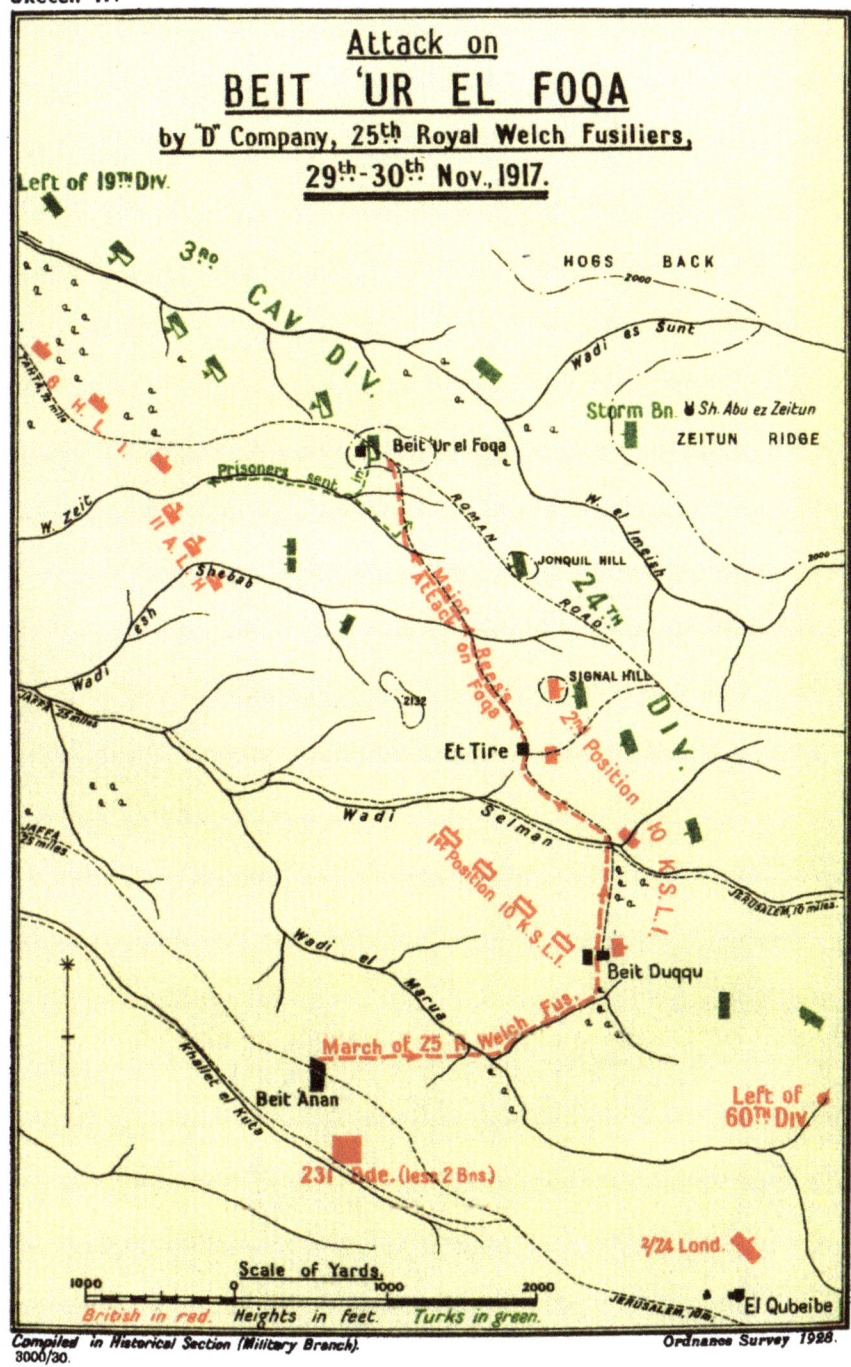

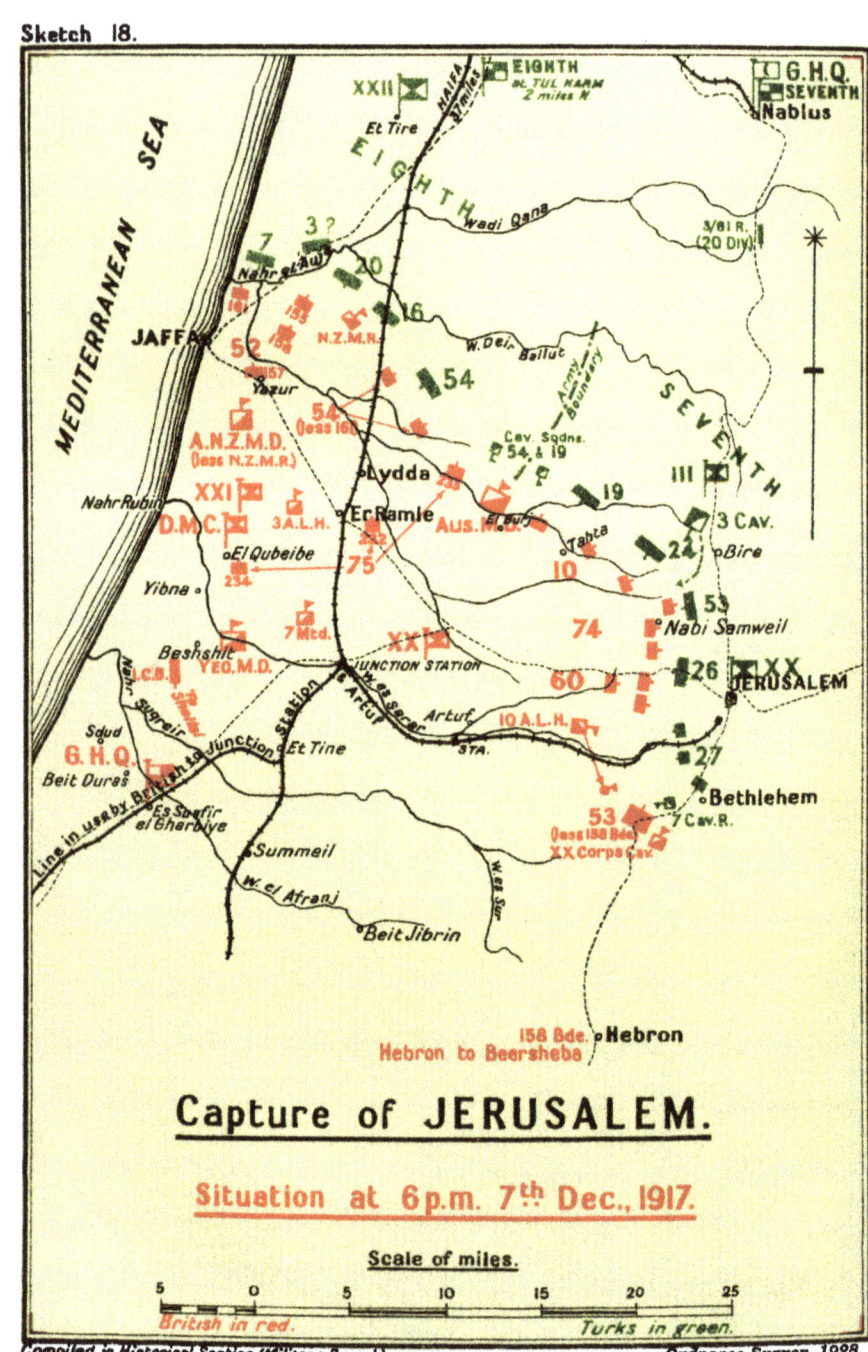

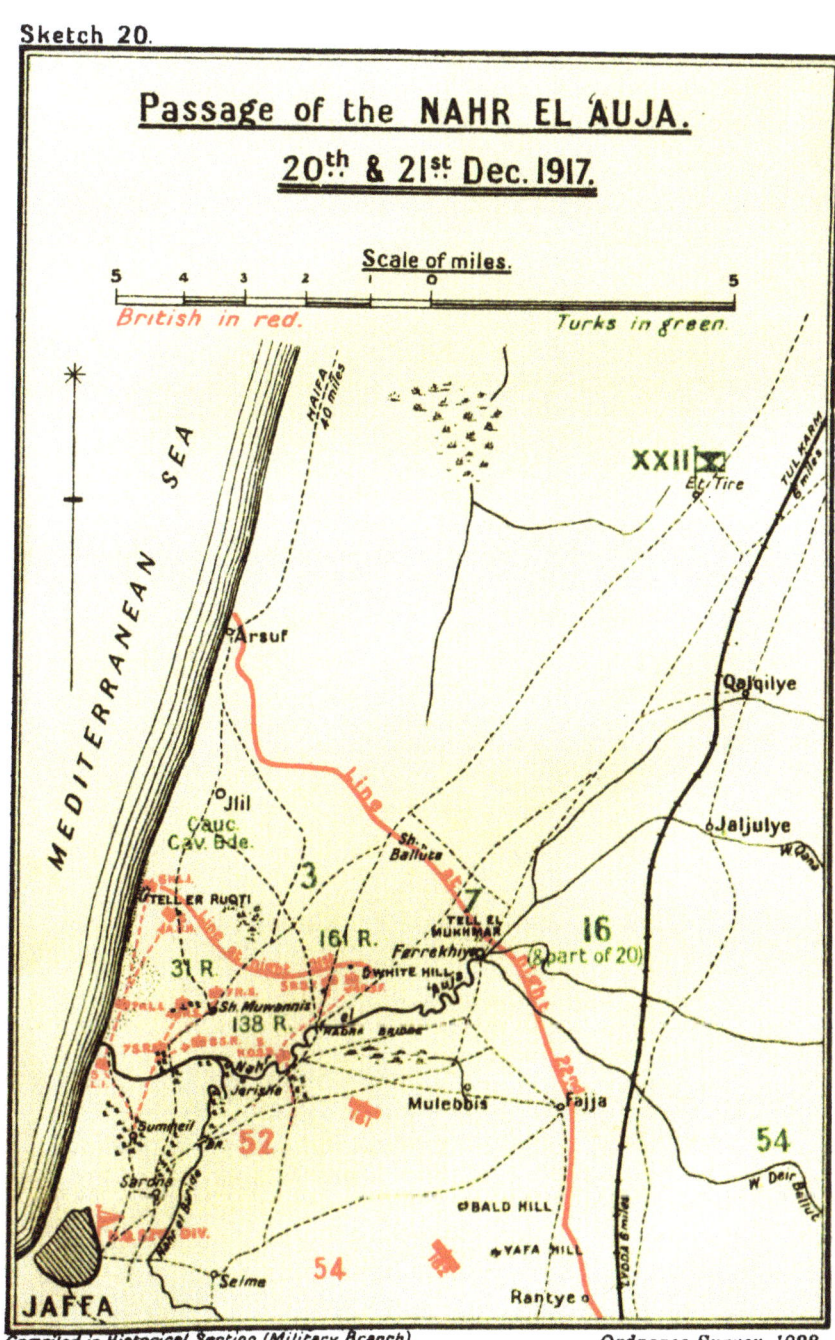

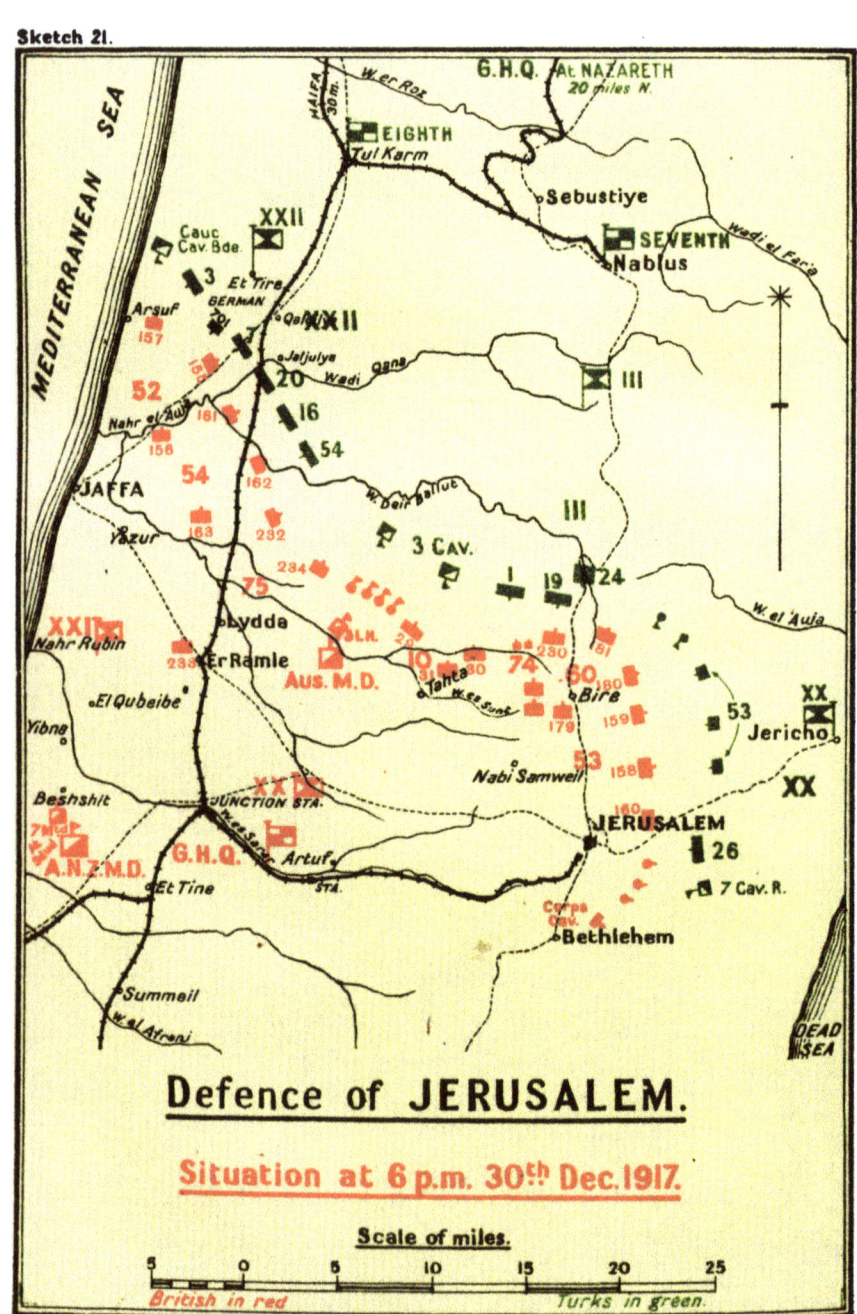

Sketch 22.

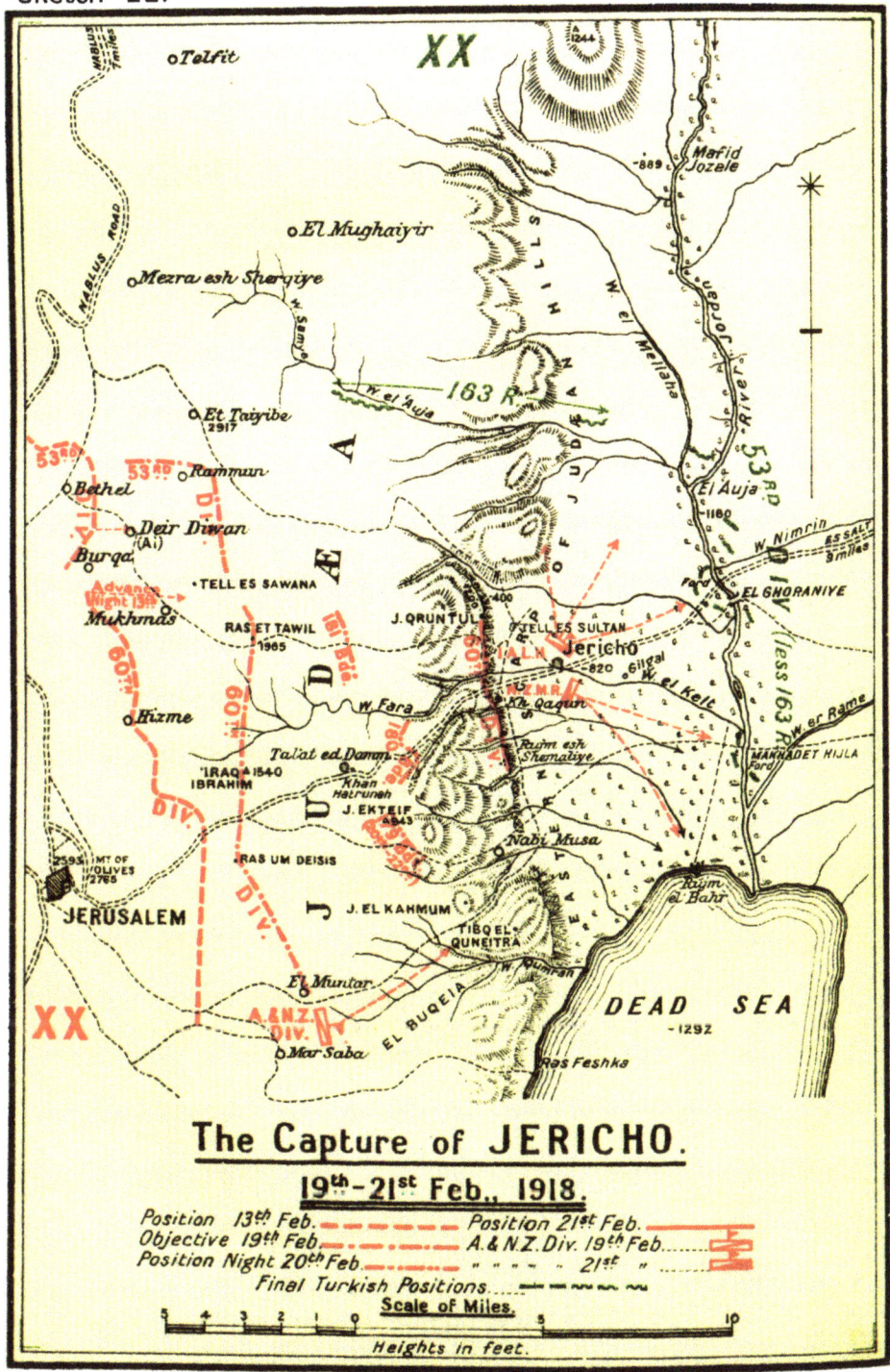

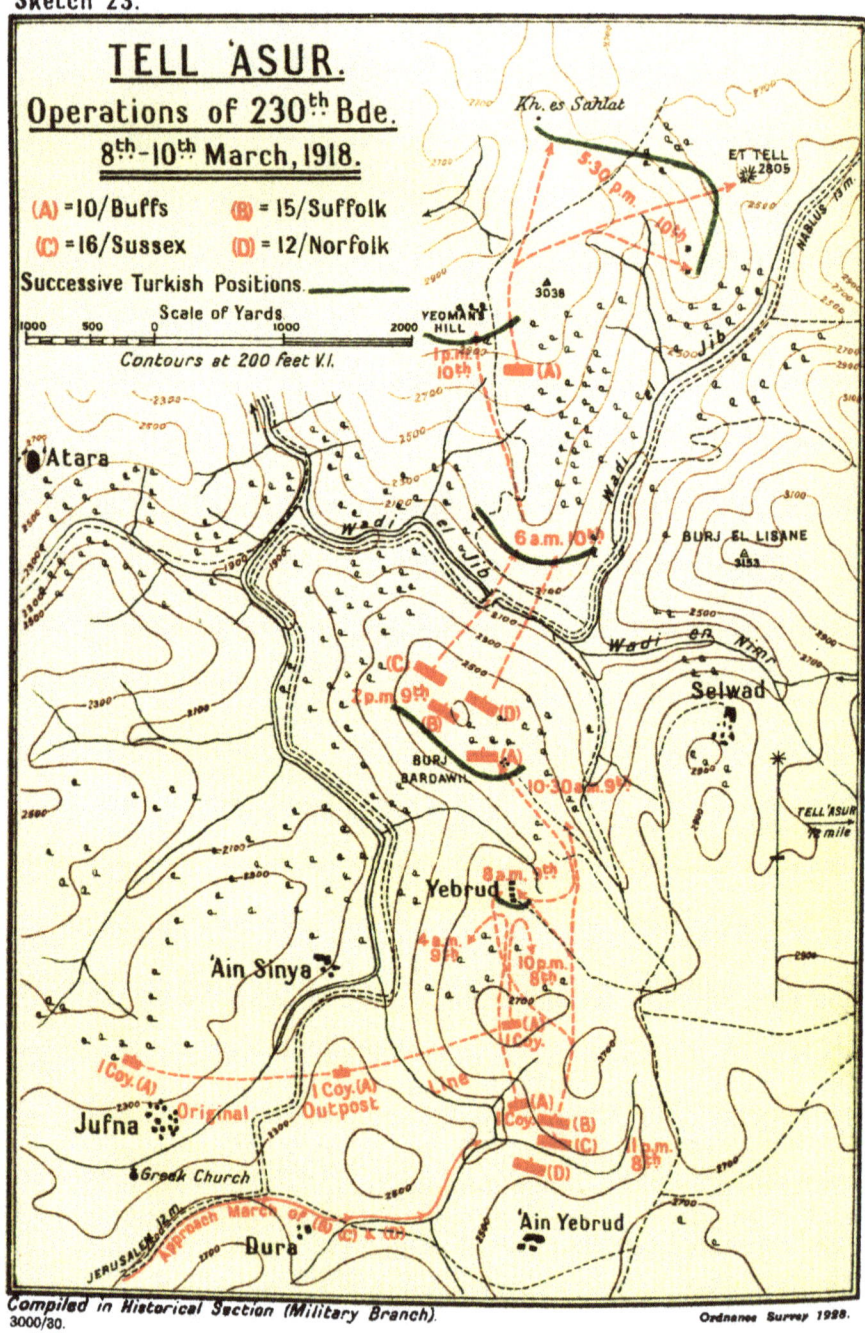

Sketch 24.

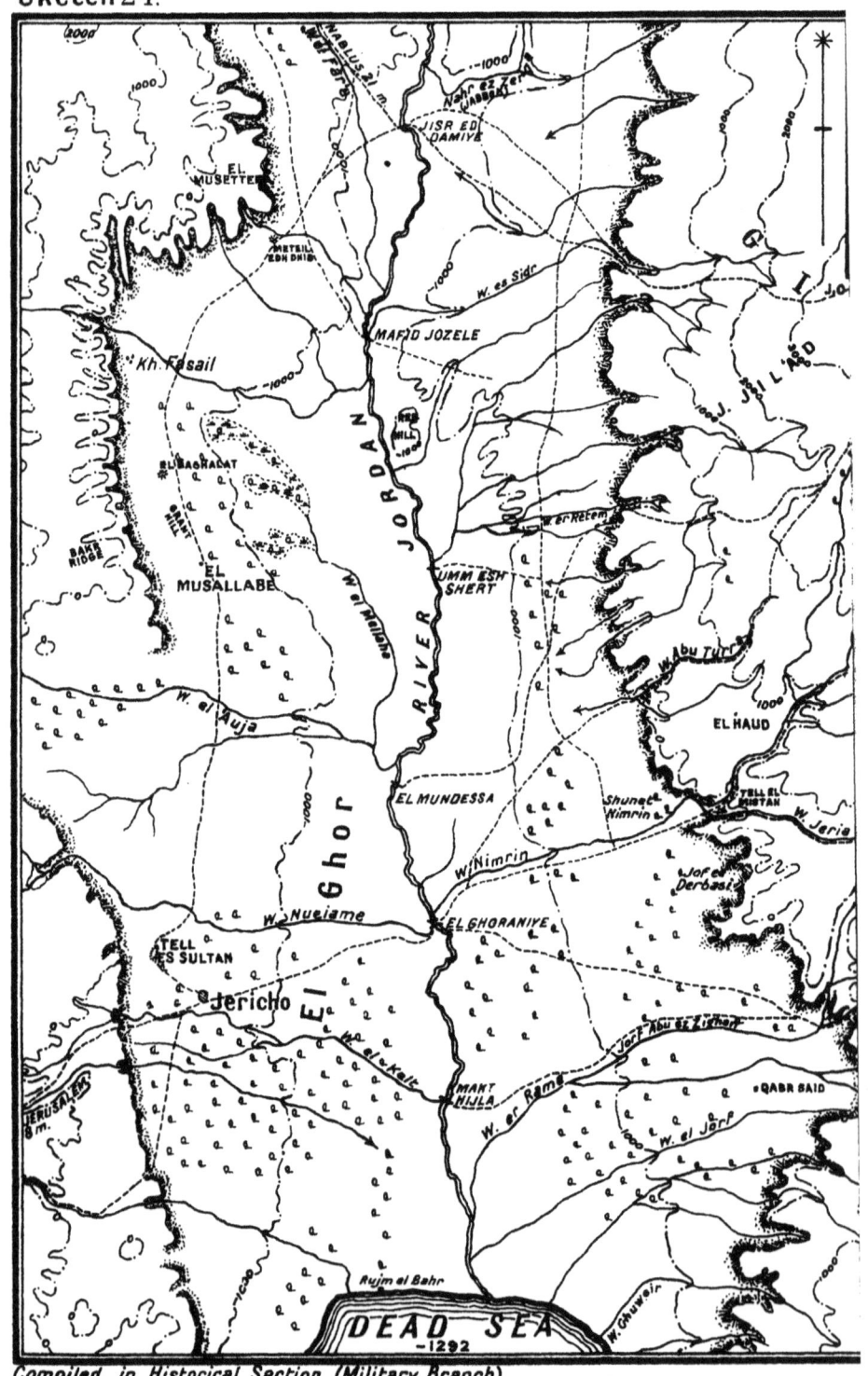

Compiled in Historical Section (Military Branch).

Theatre of Operations in TRANS-JORDAN.
(First Trans-Jordan Raid, 21st March – 2nd April; Second Trans-Jordan Raid, 30th April – 4th May; & Operations of Chaytor's Force 20th–29th September, 1918.).

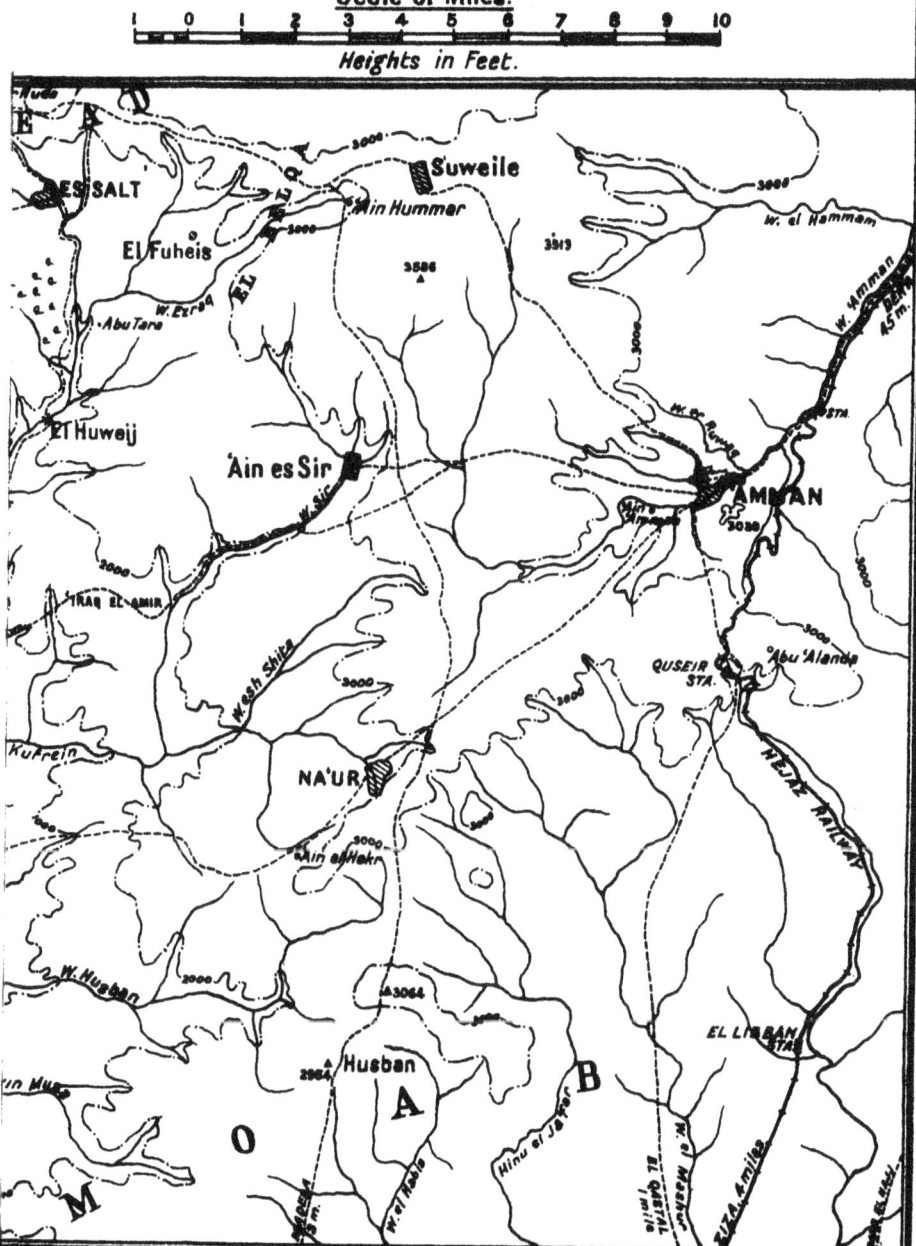

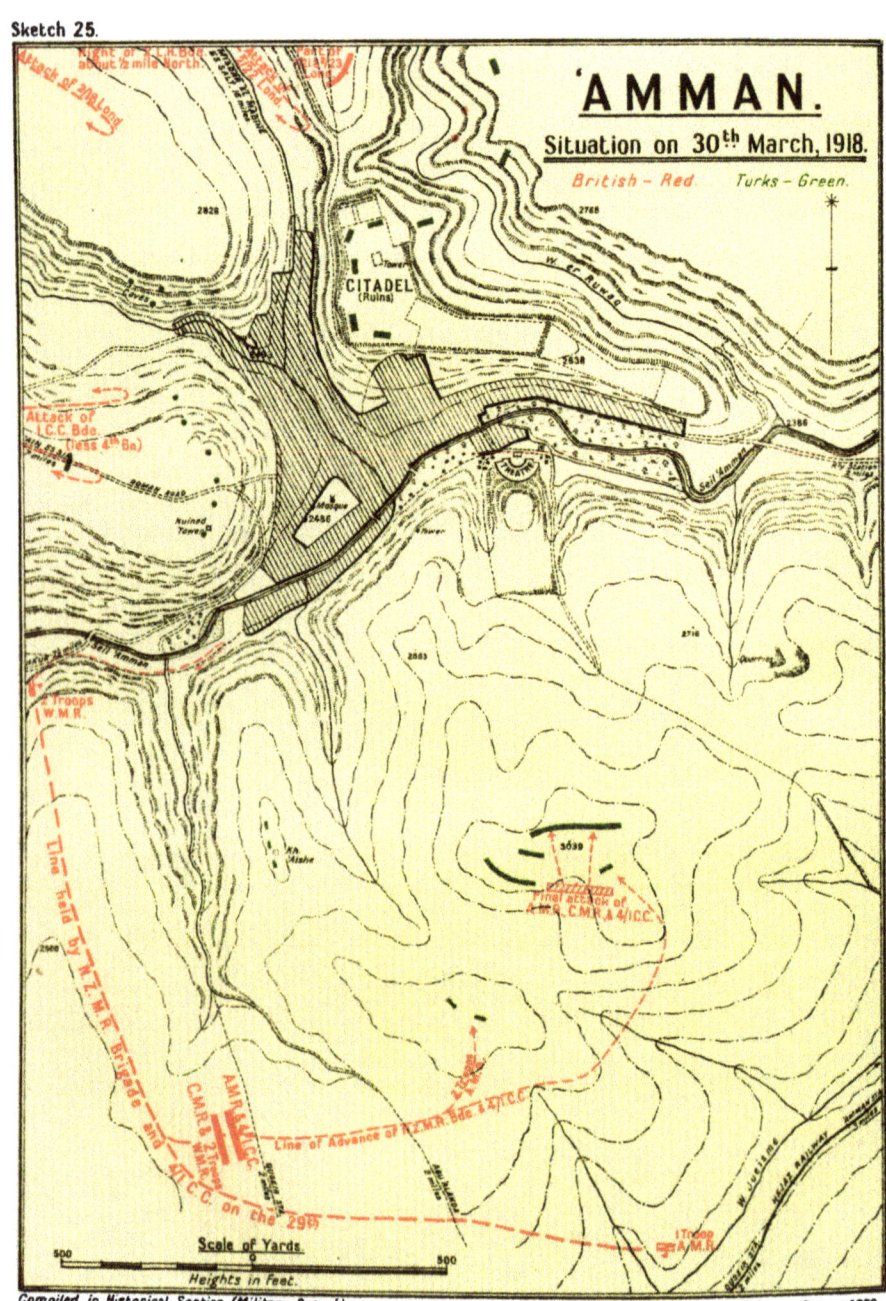

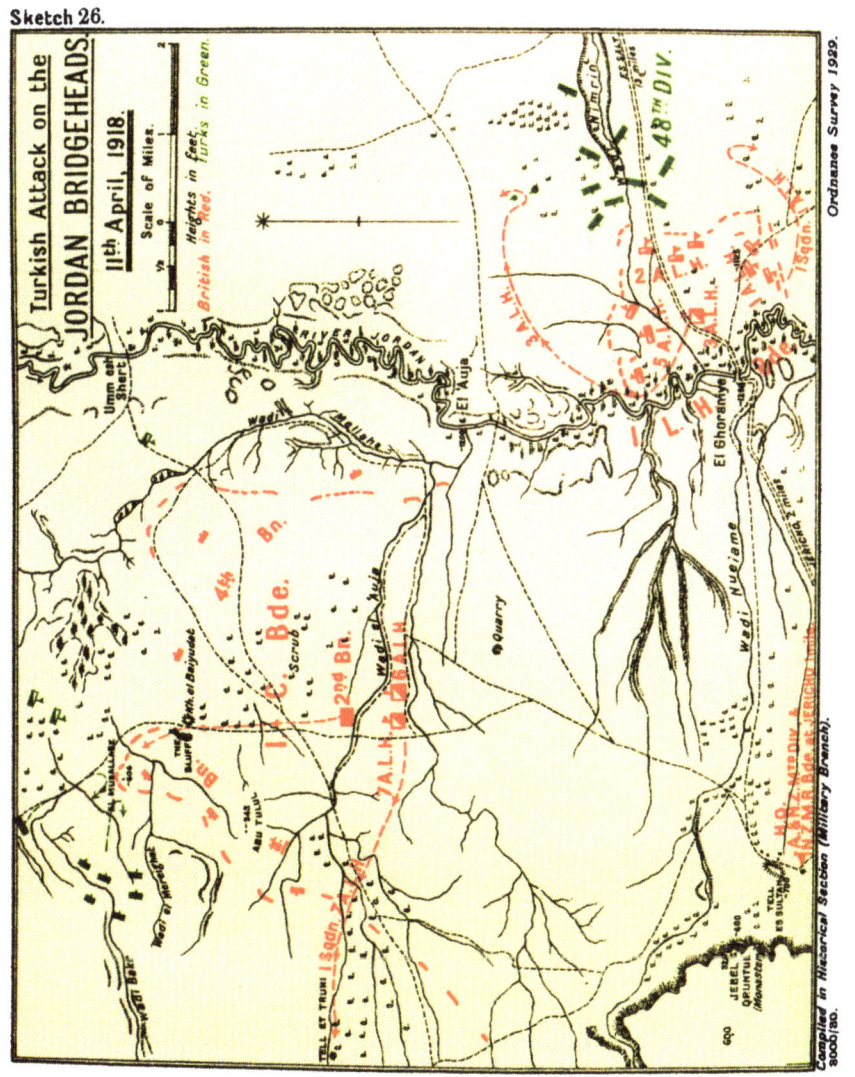

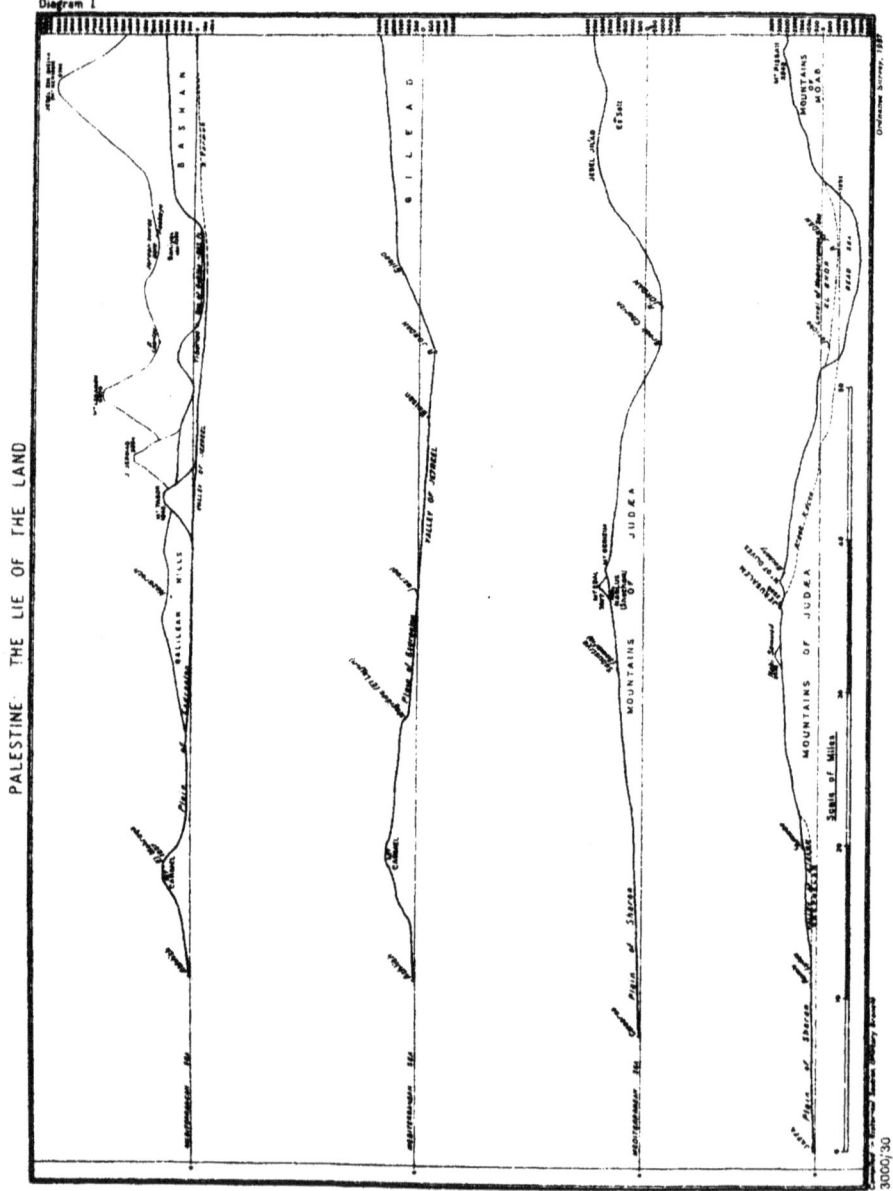

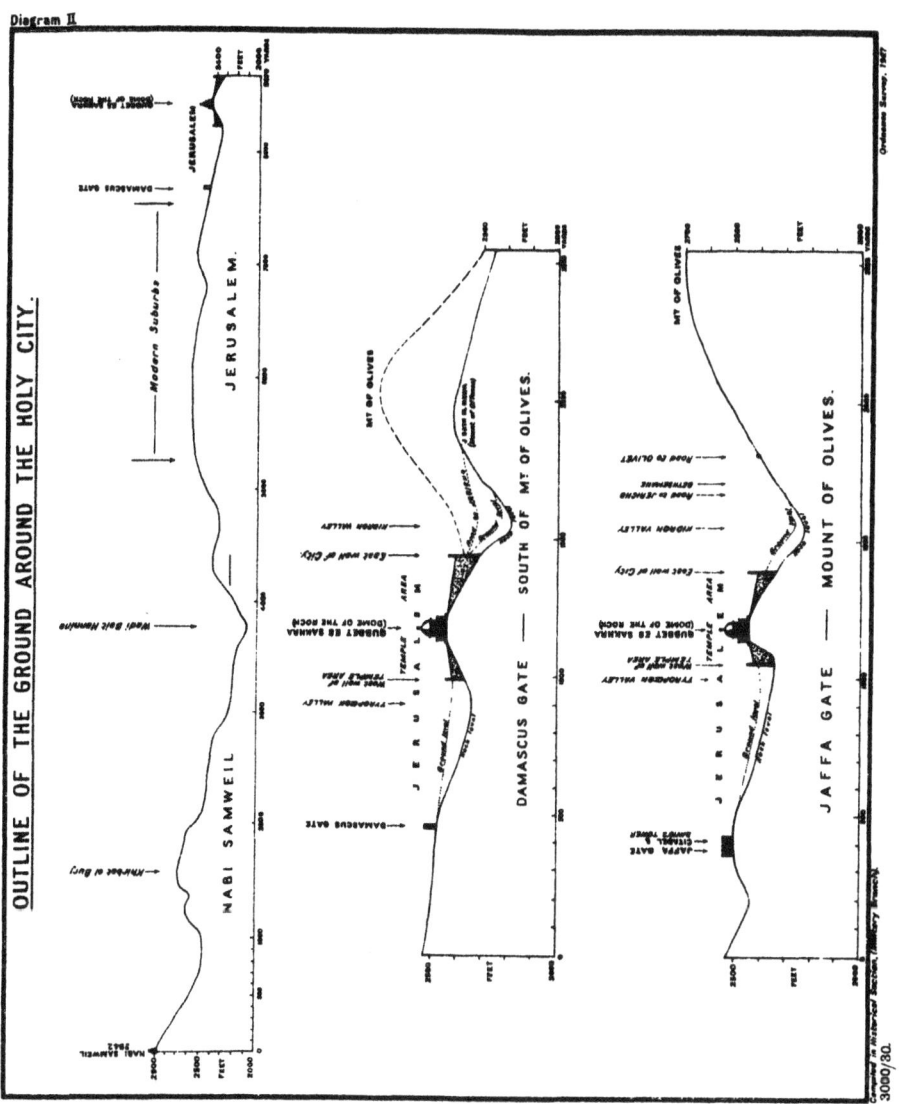

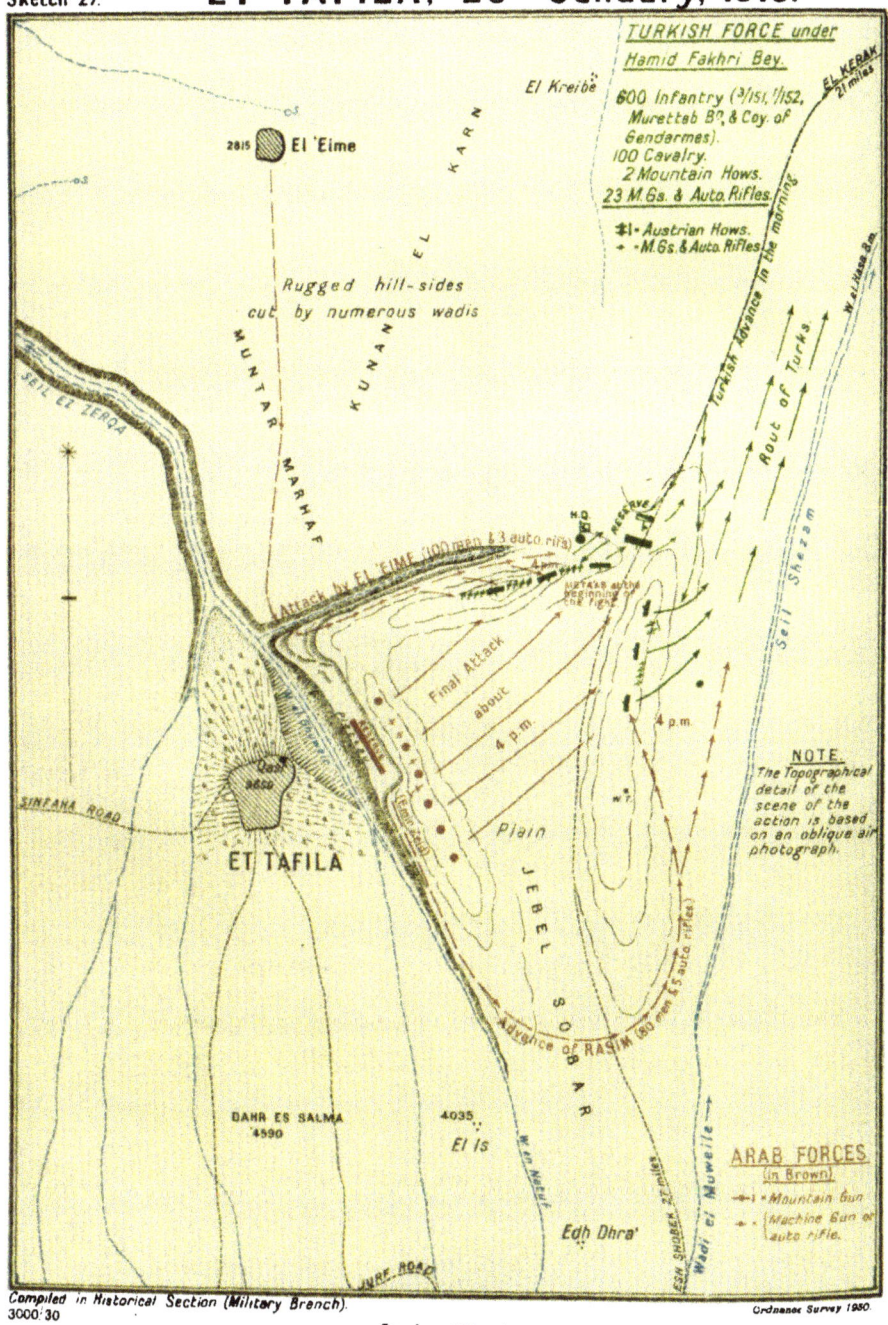

Sketch 28.

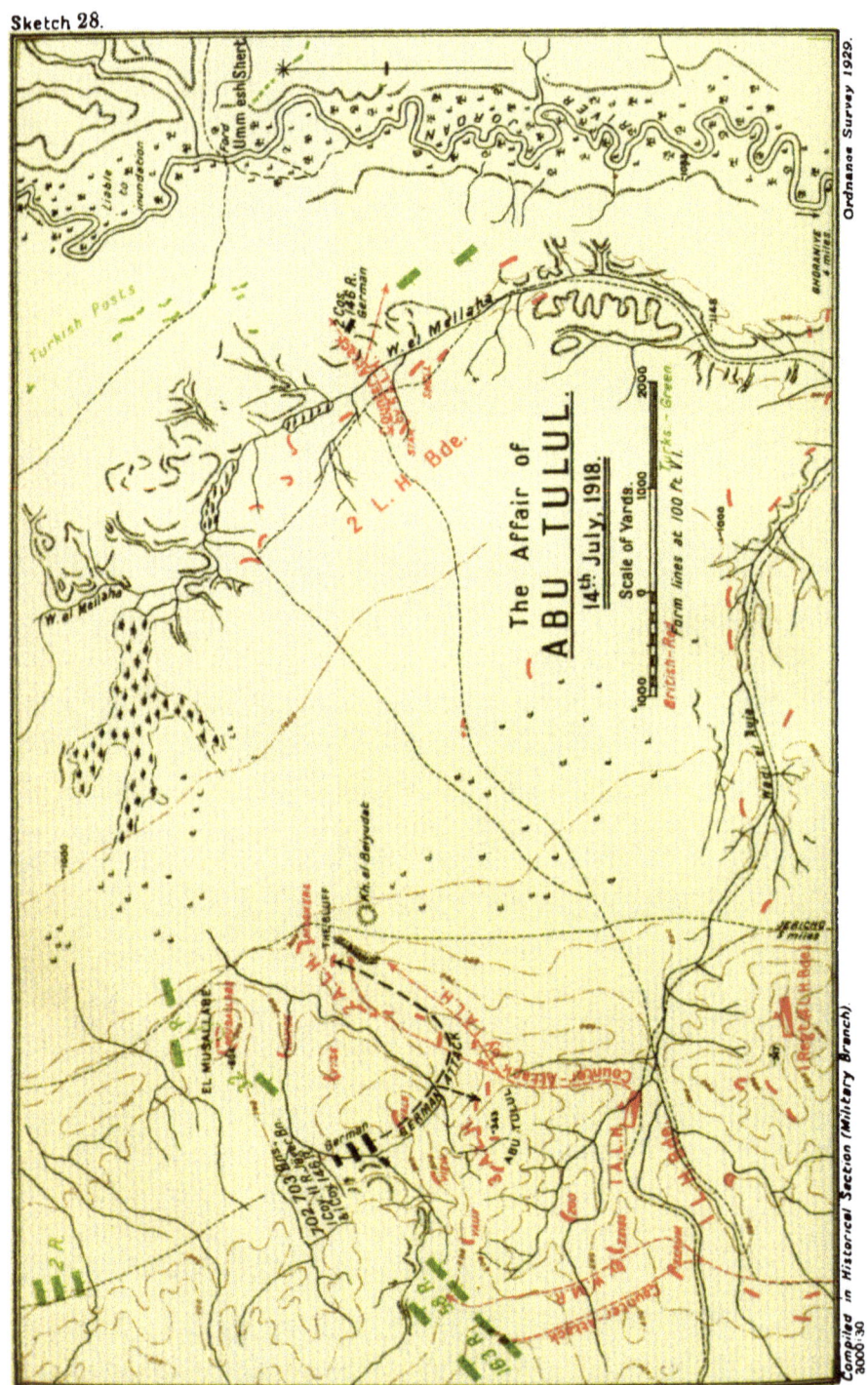

Sketch 29.

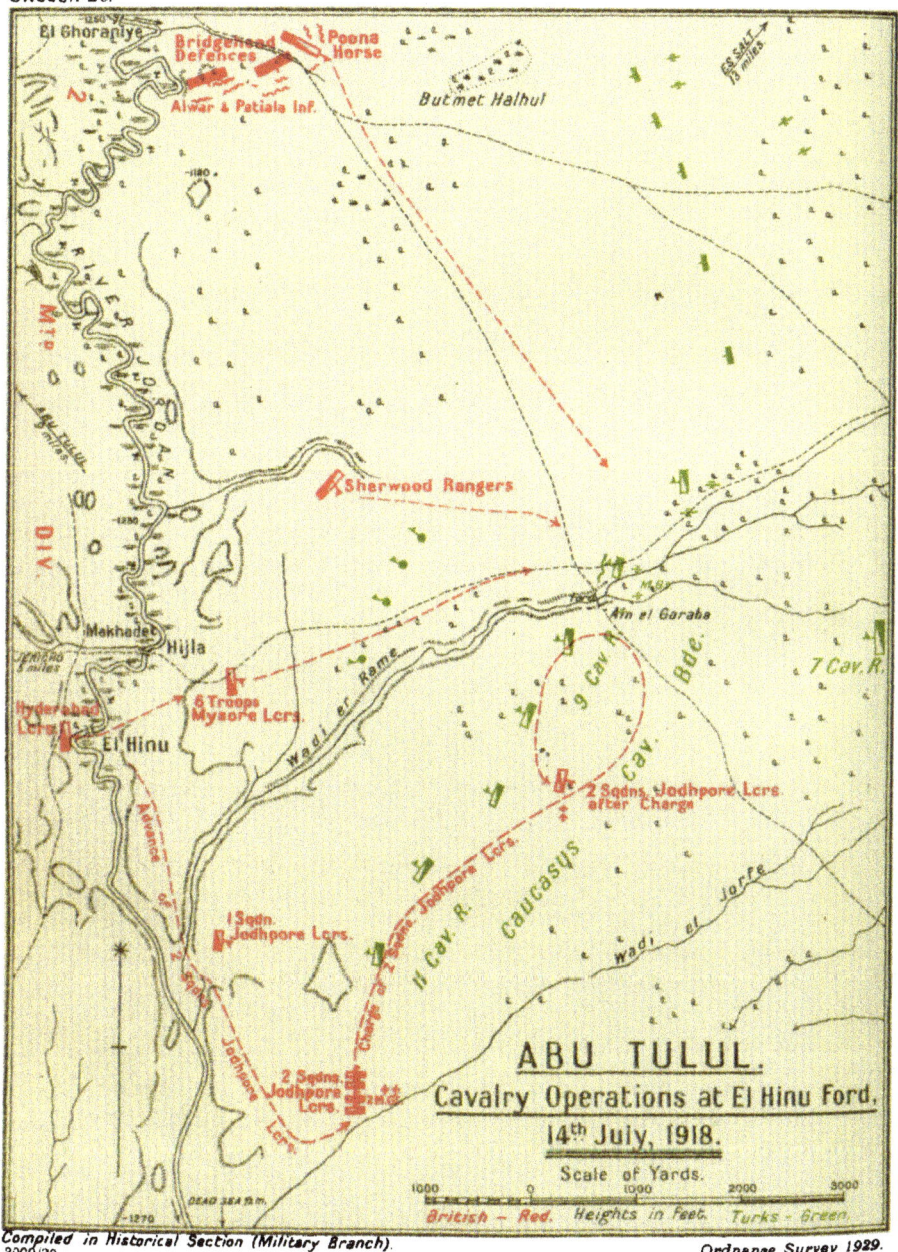

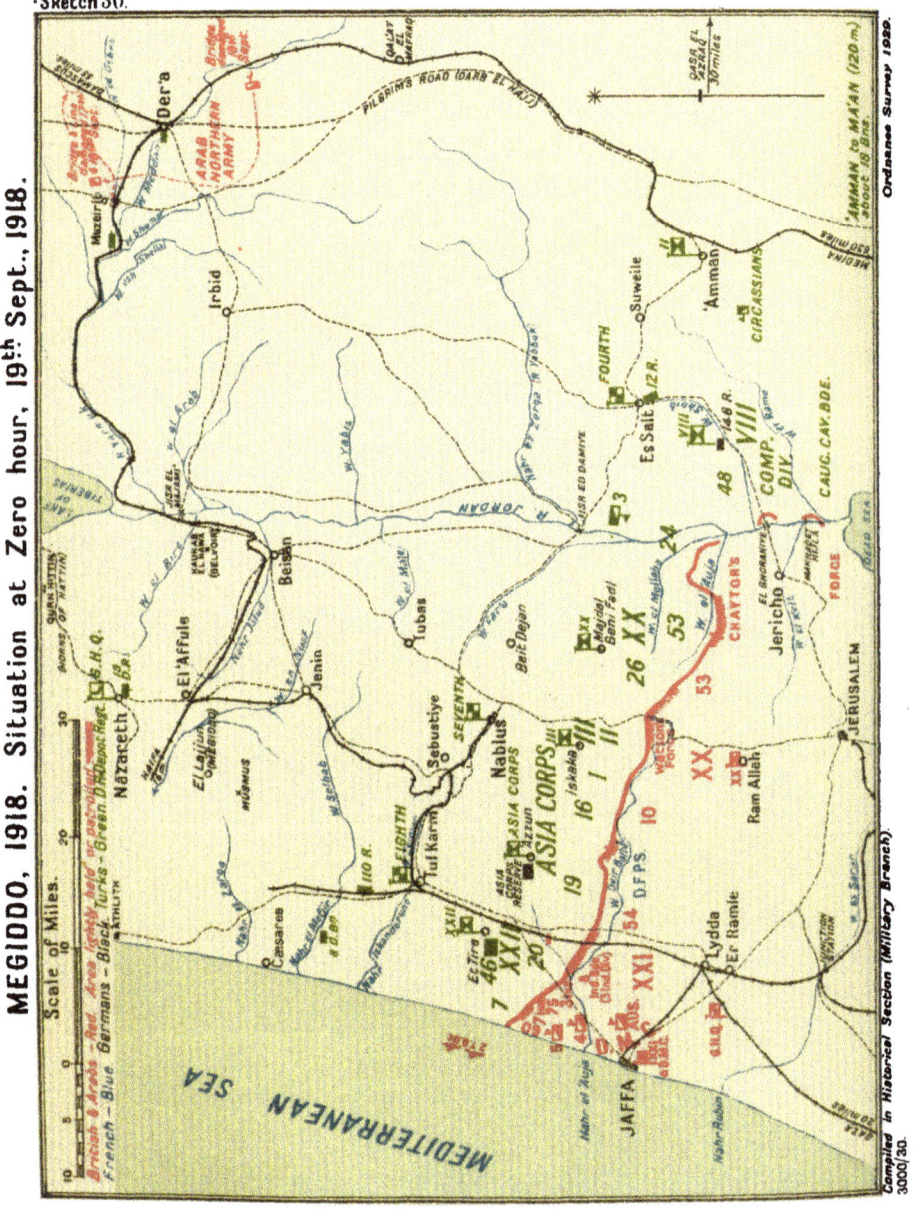

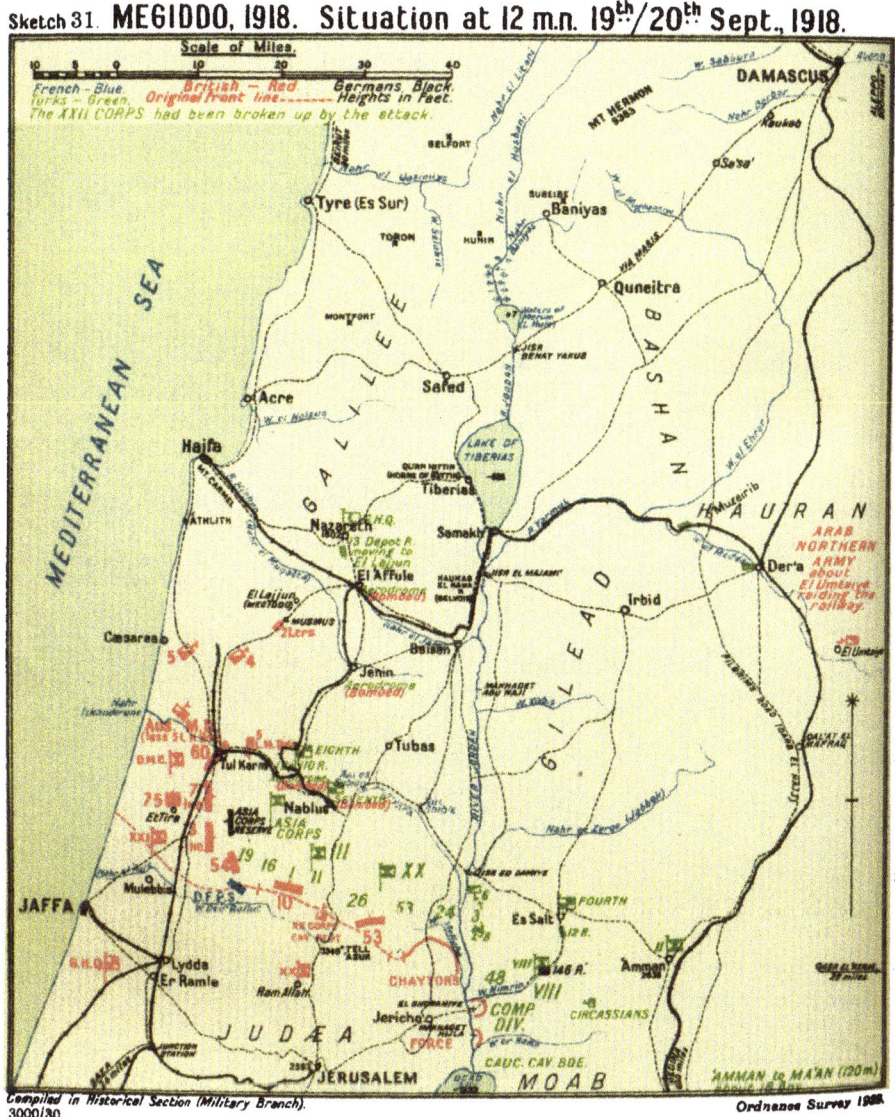
Sketch 31. MEGIDDO, 1918. Situation at 12 m.n. 19th/20th Sept., 1918.

Sketch 32. **MEGIDDO, 1918. Situation at 9 p.m. 20th Sept., 1918.**

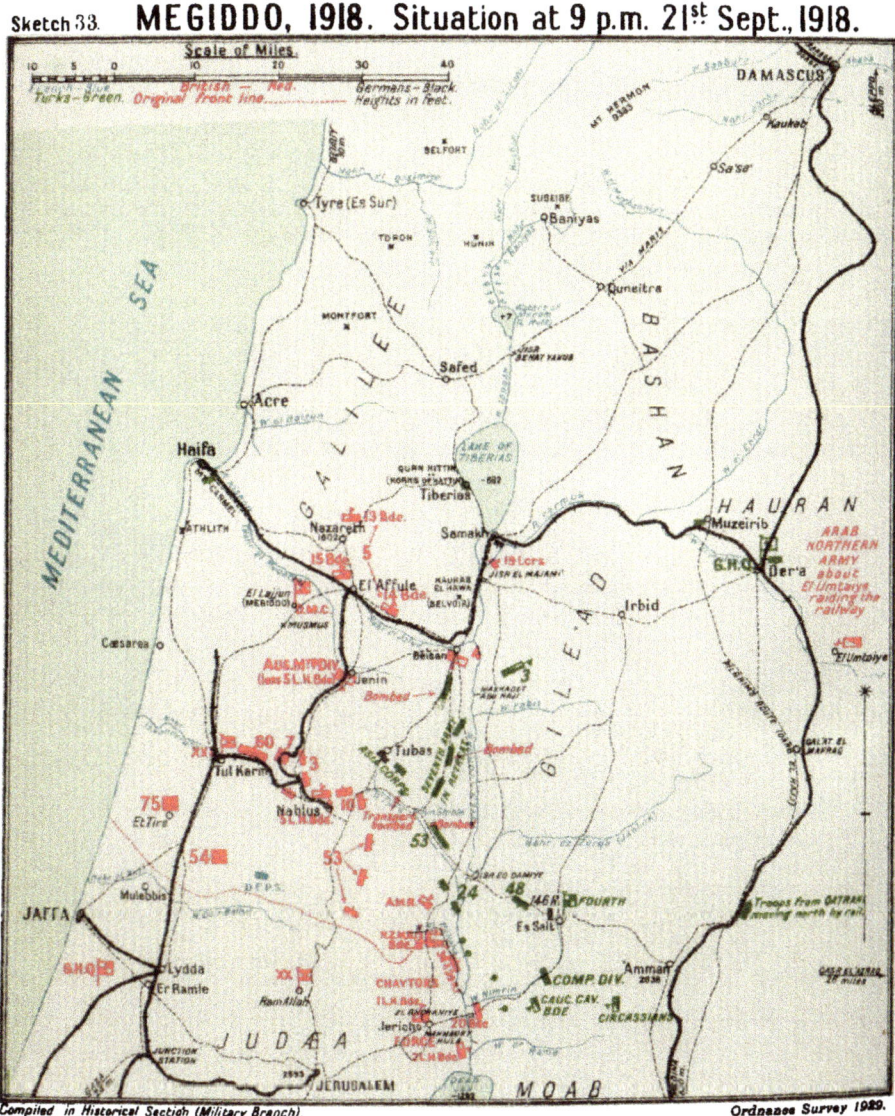

Sketch 33. MEGIDDO, 1918. Situation at 9 p.m. 21st Sept., 1918.

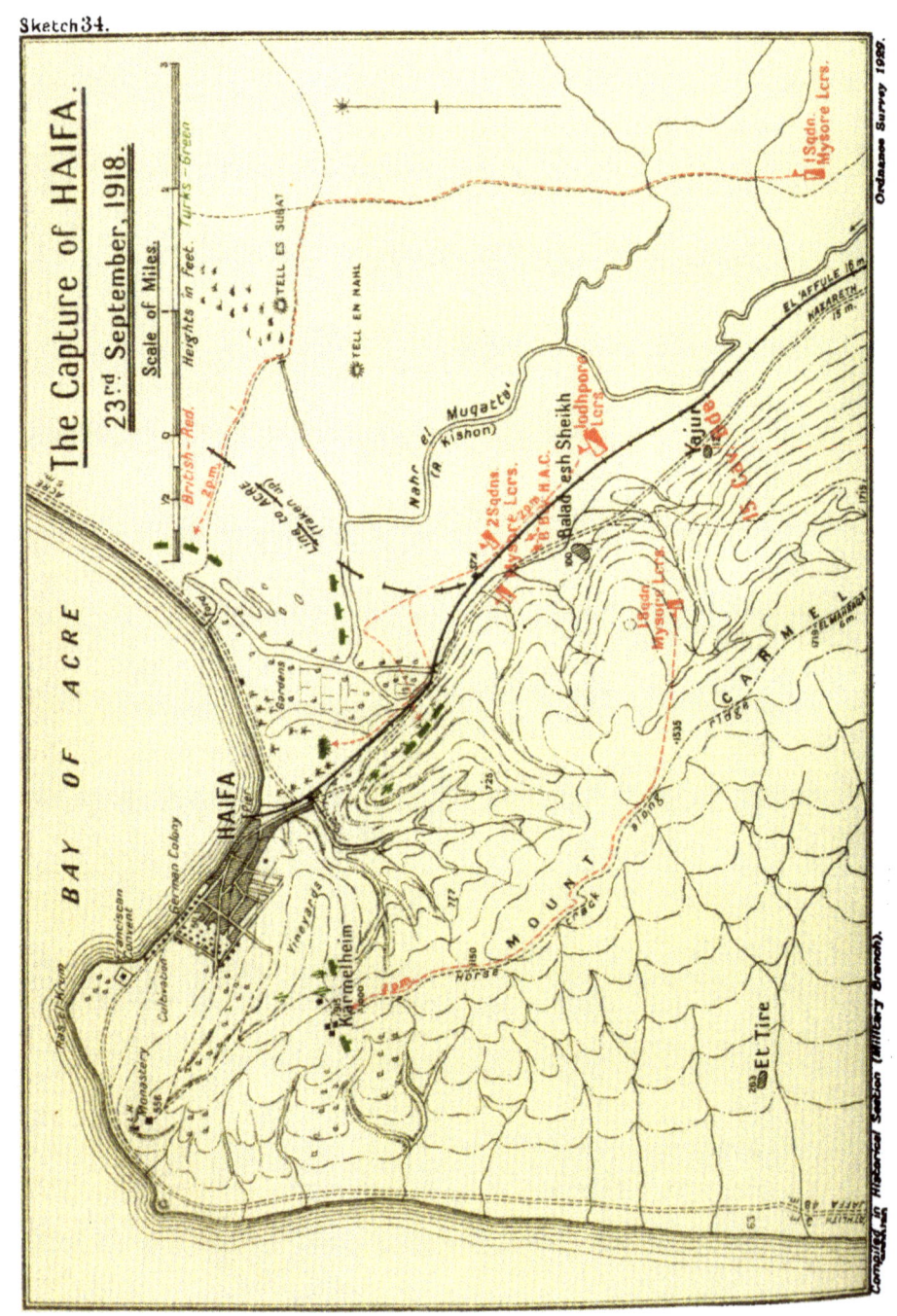

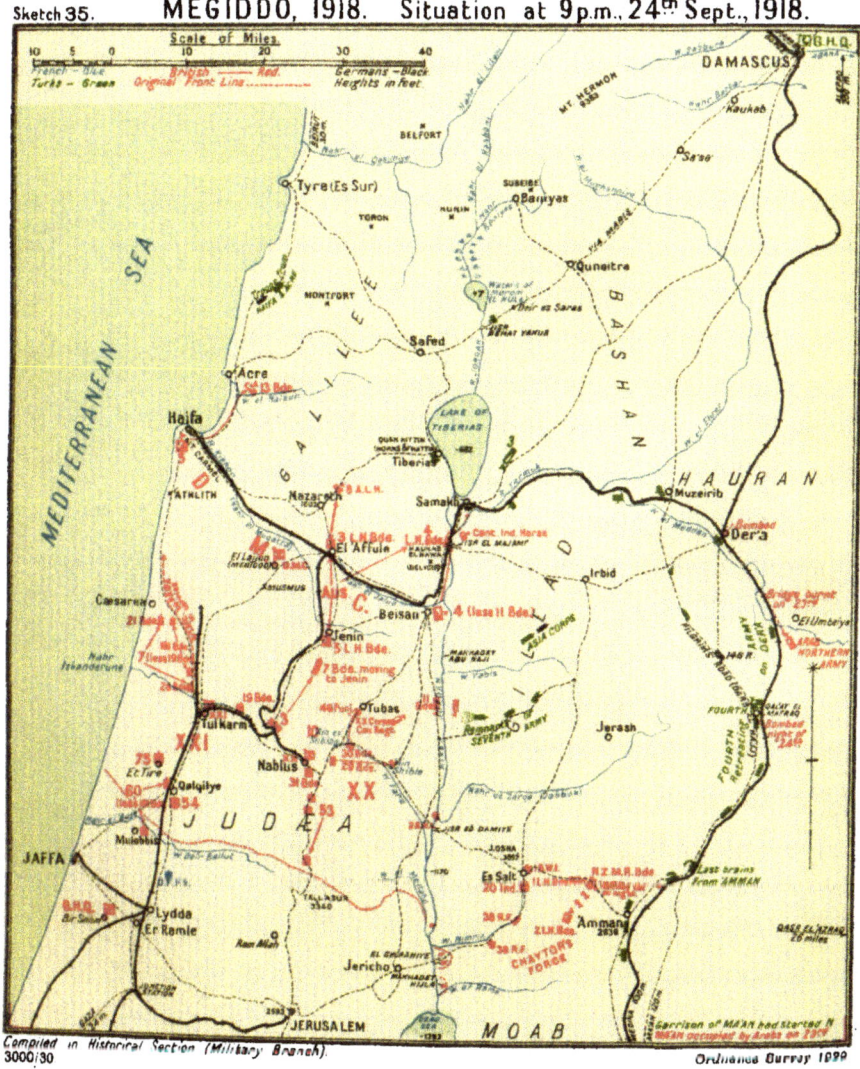

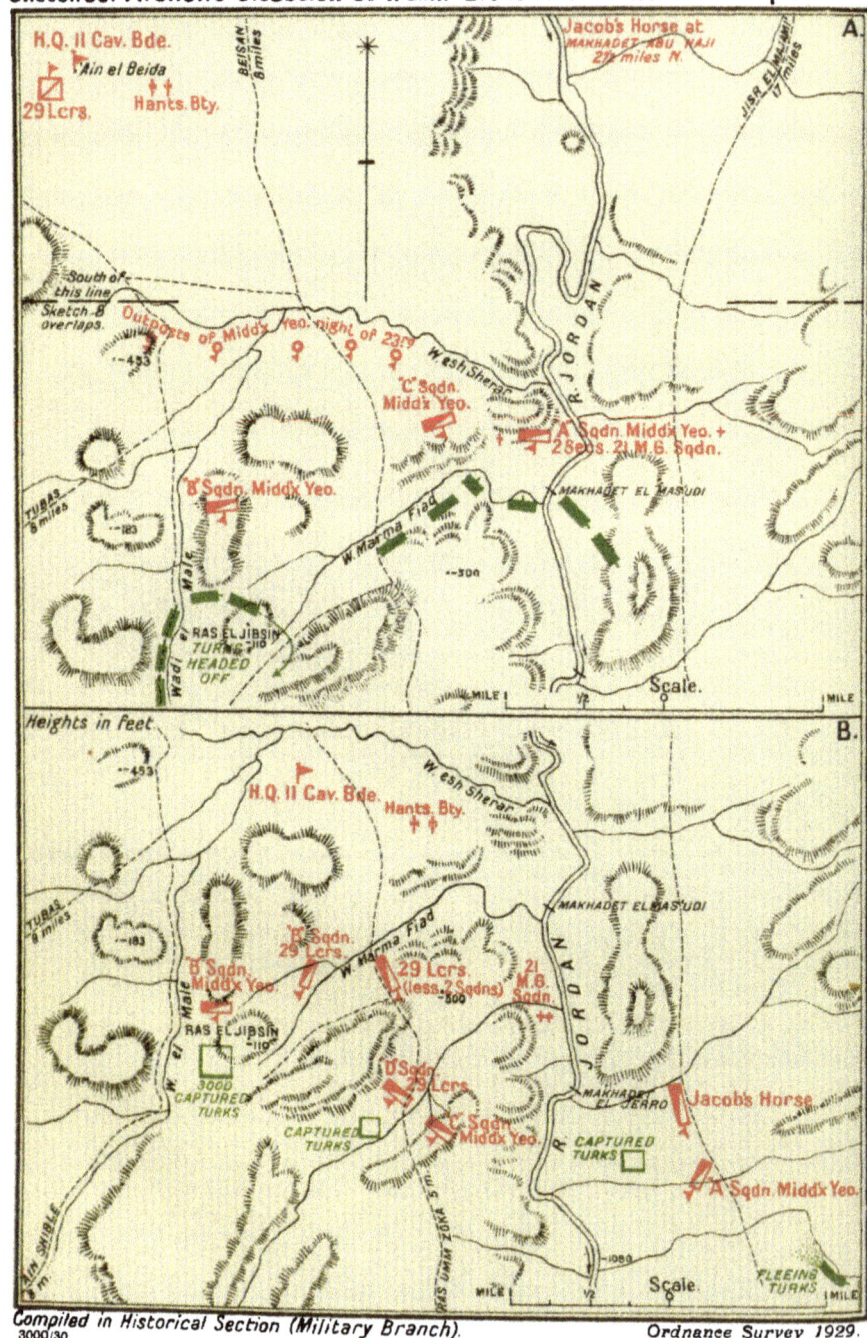

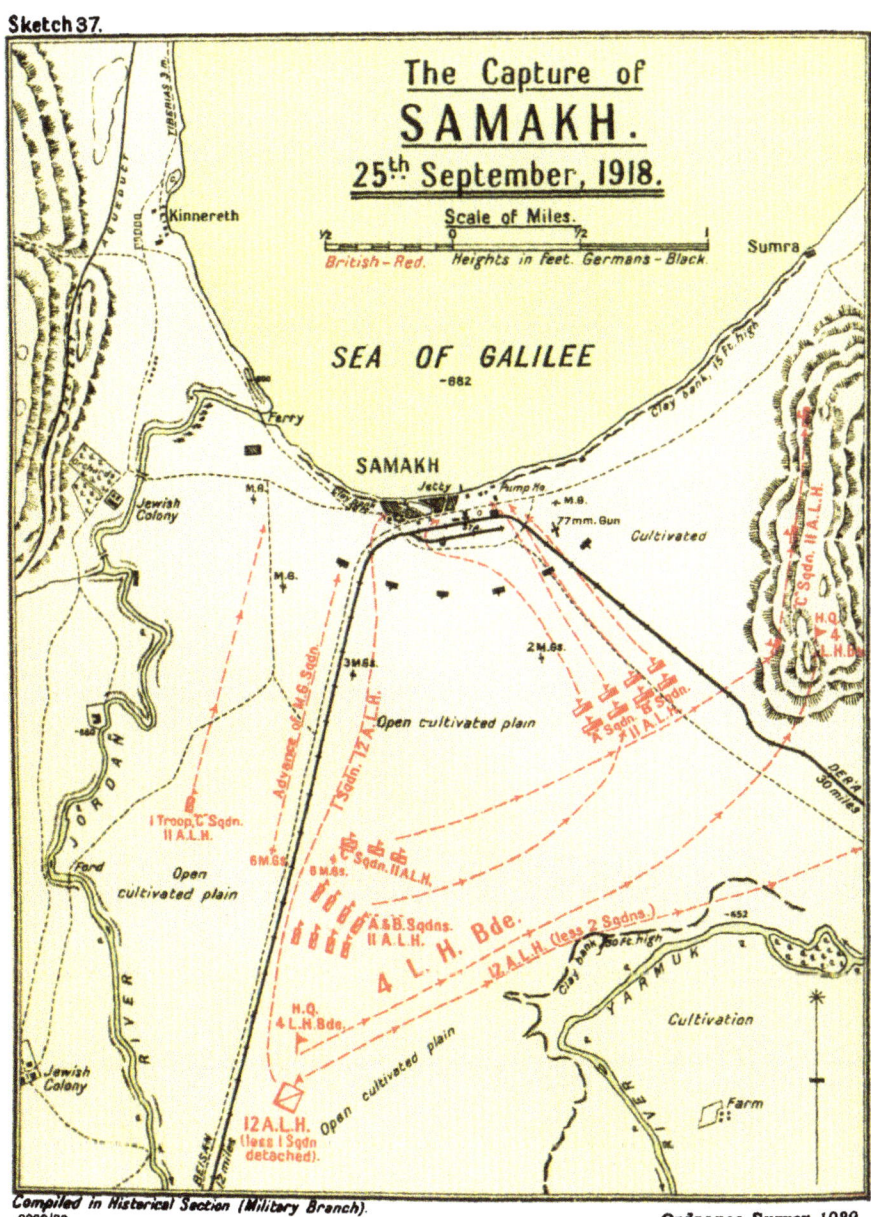

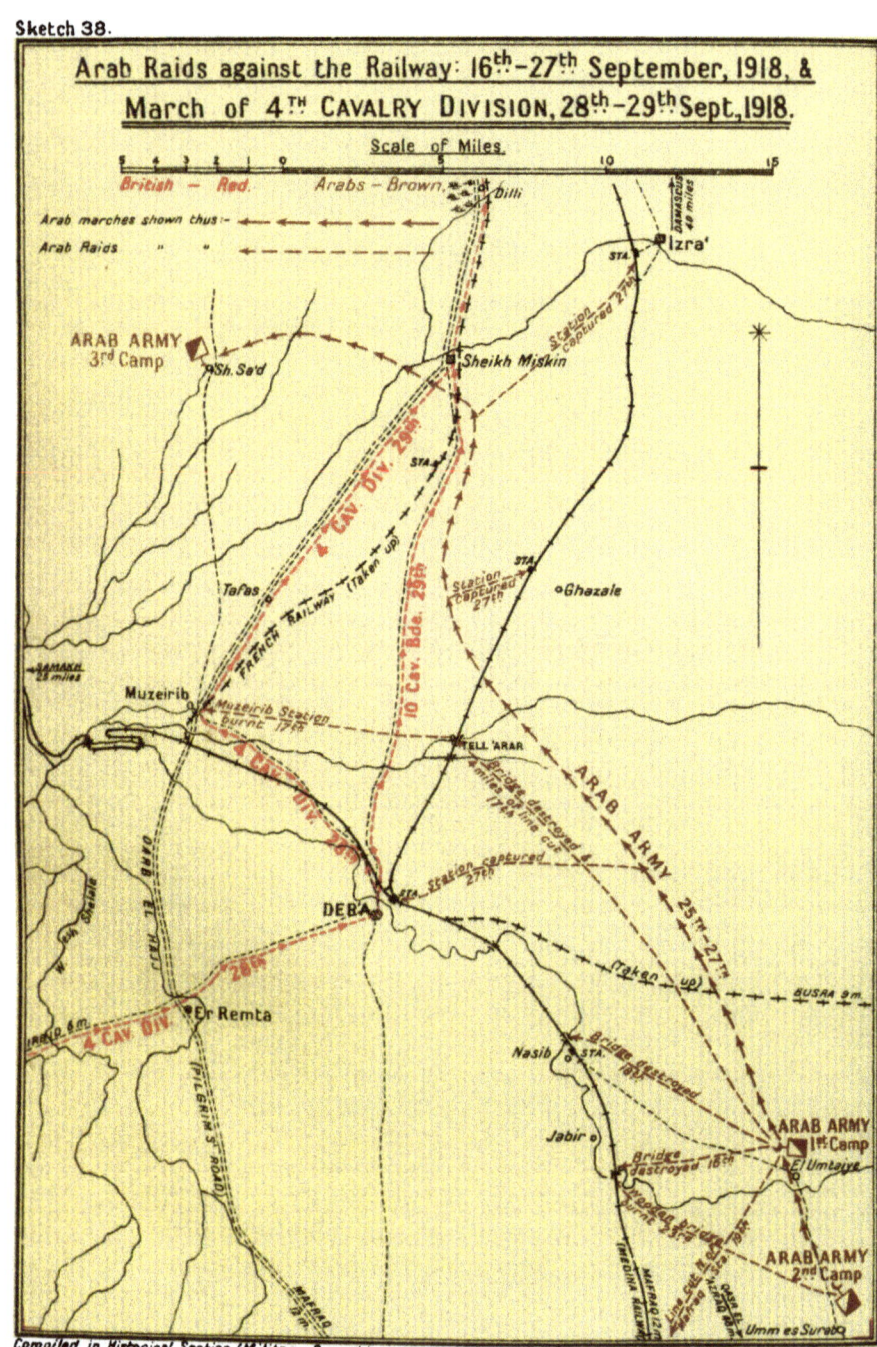

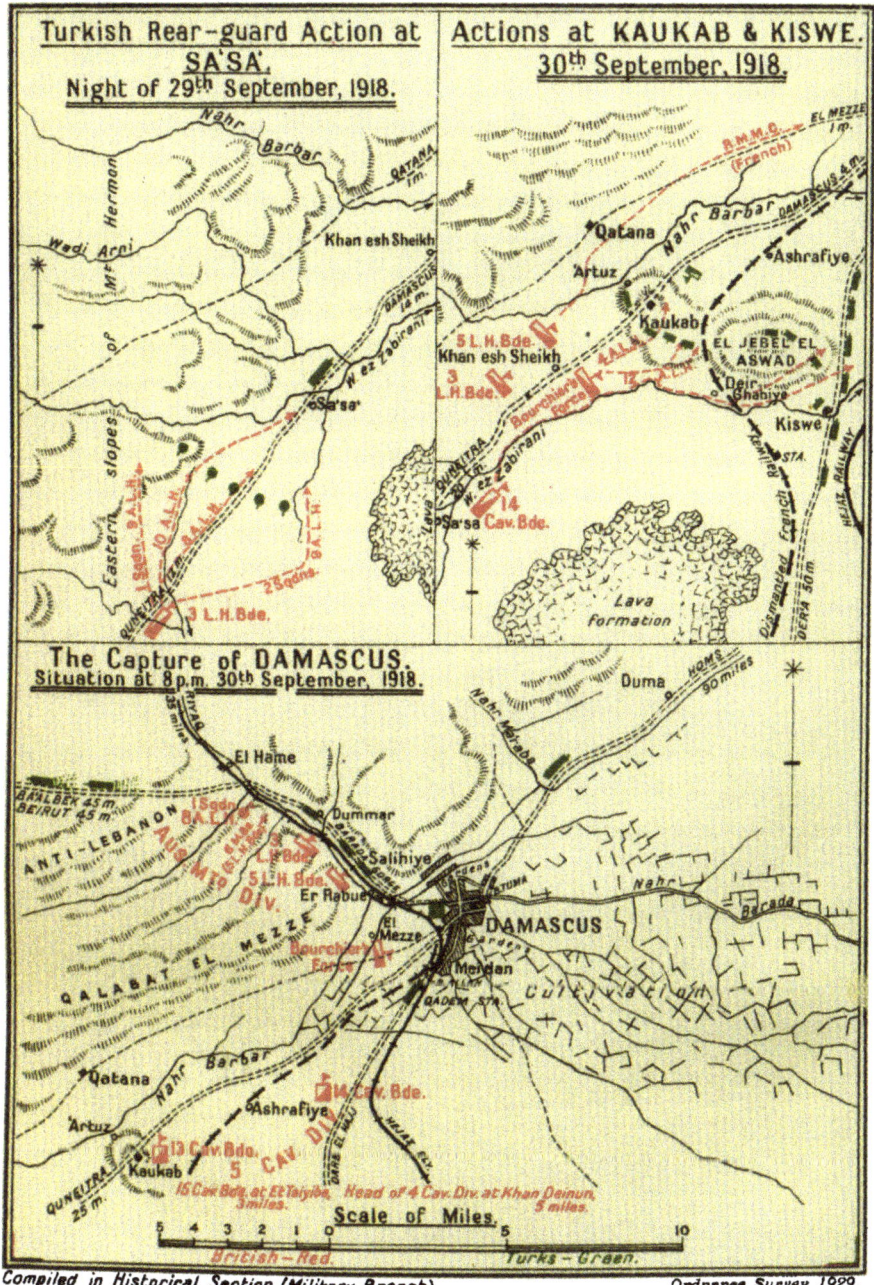

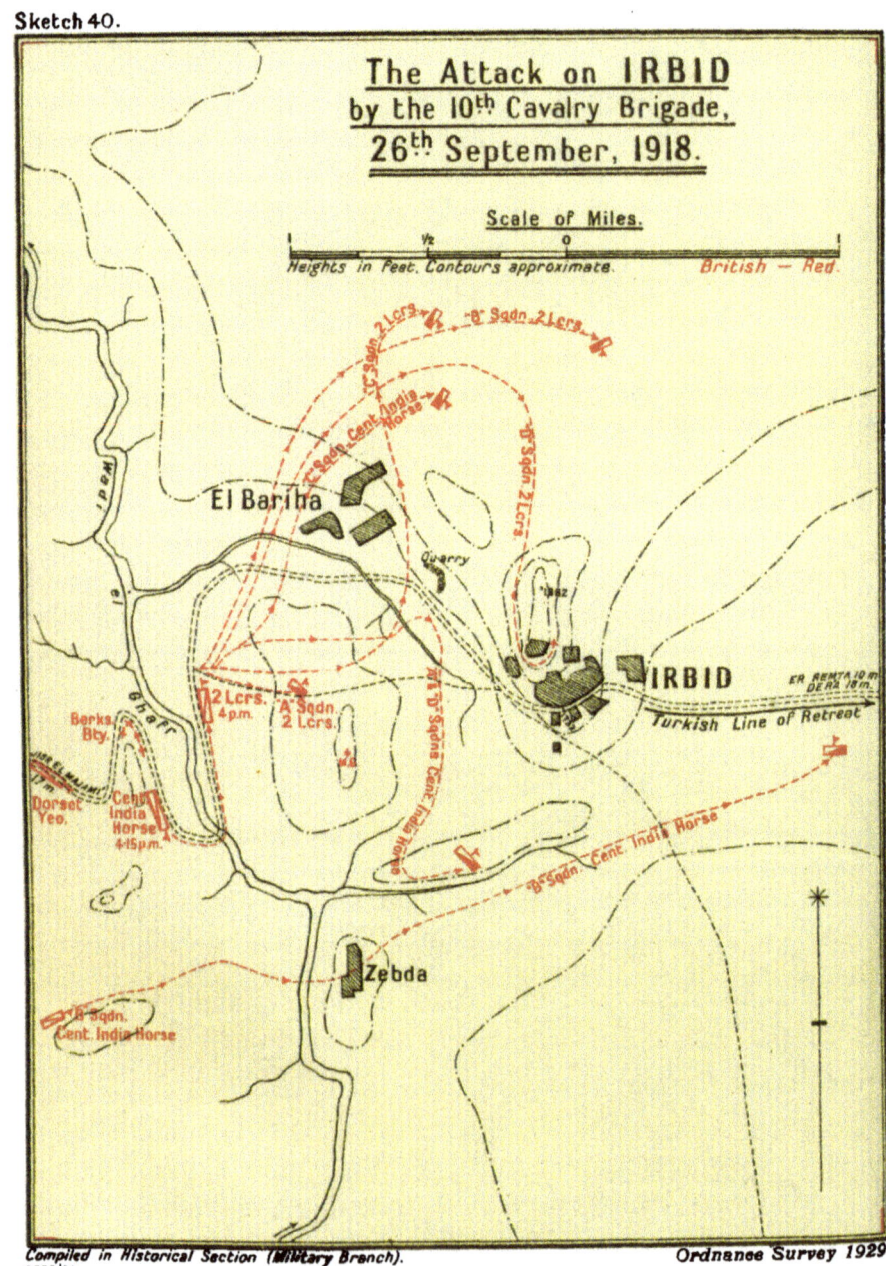

Sketch 42.

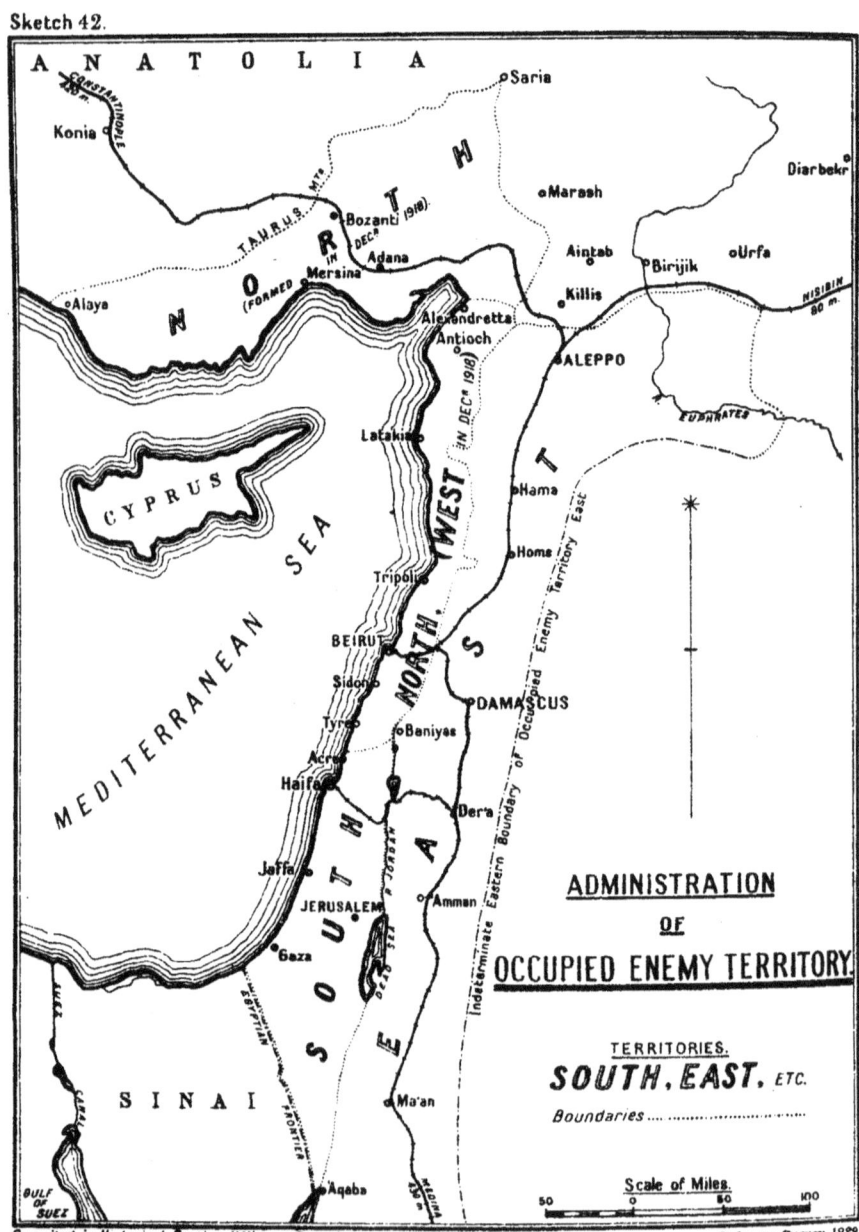

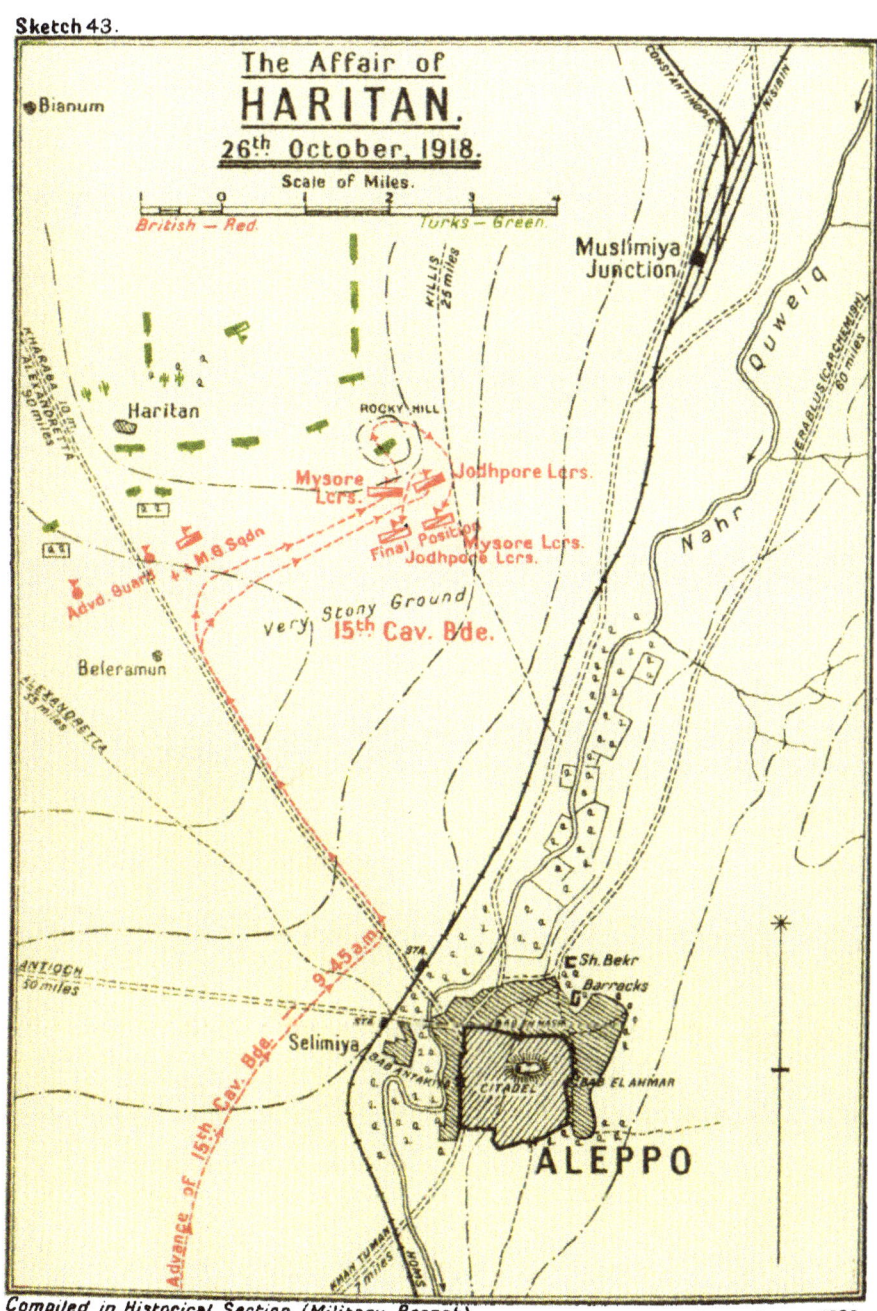

www.ingramcontent.com/pod-product-compliance
Lightning Source LLC
Chambersburg PA
CBHW040258170426
43192CB00020B/2845